Anxious Attachment Workbook for Women

Healing Your Inner Child and Overcoming Insecurity and Abandonment Fears

Isabella Cruz

The more anxiously attached we are, the more we confuse love with the anxiety of losing it." — Diane Poole Heller

This book is a work of non-fiction and is based on the research and experiences of the author. Some individuals' names and personal details have been changed to protect their privacy.

Acknowledgement

I am deeply grateful to Dr. Read Stevenson, my mentor and a brilliant psychiatrist, for his guidance throughout this journey. To Dr. Jenny White, my dear friend and psychologist, your resourcefulness has been invaluable.

A heartfelt thank you to my incredible research team, Joel and Craig, for your unwavering support and dedication.

Lastly, to my loving husband David and our daughter Bella, your love and encouragement have been my greatest source of strength. I couldn't have done this without you.

With heartfelt thanks,

Isabella Cruz

About the Author

Isabella Cruz is a renowned psychologist and resilience coach, known for her empowering and relatable approach to mental health. Holding a doctorate in Psychology from Stanford University, she specializes in cognitive-behavioral therapy and mindfulness techniques.

With extensive experience in clinical practice, Isabella has dedicated her career to helping individuals overcome mental barriers and achieve emotional freedom. She lives in Seattle, where she continues to inspire and support others through her practice, coaching, and public speaking.

Other Books by this same author includes:

Table Of Contents

How To Use This Workbook

Start with Self-Reflection: Begin by setting aside some quiet time to reflect on your personal experiences with attachment. This will help you connect with the material on a deeper level.

Read Each Chapter Carefully: Work through each chapter at your own pace. Take your time to understand the concepts and how they apply to your life.

Complete the Exercises: After reading, engage with the exercises provided. They are designed to help you explore your thoughts, emotions, and behaviors related to avoidant attachment.

Journal Your Thoughts: Use the space provided to jot down your thoughts, insights, and any patterns you notice as you work through the exercises.

Practice Consistently: Consistency is key. Set aside regular time each week to work on the exercises, even if it's just a few minutes a day.

Reflect and Review: Periodically, go back and review your notes and completed exercises. Reflect on your progress and how your understanding of avoidant attachment has evolved.

Apply What You Learn: Begin to apply the insights and strategies you've gained in your daily life. Notice how your relationships and interactions change as you grow.

Revisit as Needed: This workbook is a tool for ongoing growth. Feel free to revisit sections as your understanding deepens or as new challenges arise.

Sometimes our anxiety comes not from fear of being alone, but from fear of being unloved. — Stephanie Dowrick

Introduction

Pearl came to me as a client a few years ago. She was a high-achieving lawyer working at a prestigious law firm in downtown Seattle. The first thing you'd notice about her was how together she seemed.

She was sharp, impeccably dressed, and carried herself with this quiet confidence that made you instantly think she had everything figured out. But as I've learned over the years, those who seem to have it all together are often the ones struggling the most inside.

Pearl's life was a relentless stream of early mornings and late nights. She would often joke about her insane work hours, but the exhaustion in her eyes betrayed her. When she first walked into my office, she wasn't looking for help with her career. No, Pearl had that down to a science.

She was there because, despite all her success, she felt utterly alone. She had never been in a serious relationship that lasted more than a few months.

Most of her friendships had drifted apart because she was "too busy." And when she wasn't working, Pearl felt this heaviness—an emptiness she couldn't quite shake.

During our first few sessions, she mostly talked about work. She seemed comfortable in that zone, telling me about the high-profile cases she was working on, the victories in court, the politics of her firm.

It was clear Pearl was a perfectionist, driven by this internal need to always be the best. But eventually, after a lot of gentle pushing, we started to explore her past, where all of this pressure was coming from.

She grew up in a household where love wasn't freely given. Her father was emotionally cold, the kind of man who thought showing affection would make his children weak. Her mother was equally distant, caught up in her own world of status and appearances.

For Pearl, love became something you earned through achievement.

She learned early on that if she brought home straight A's or won awards, she'd get a nod of approval from her father or a rare compliment from her mother. But anything less than perfection? She was met with indifference.

This mindset carried into adulthood. Pearl became a top lawyer, not because she loved the law, but because she craved that sense of approval she had never fully received as a child. But with her parents both gone now,

Pearl was left chasing after something she couldn't quite name. She thought that by being the best in her field, by being indispensable at work, she'd finally feel worthy of love. But all it left her with was exhaustion and loneliness.

One day, Pearl came into my office after winning a big case. She had been working on it for months—countless late nights, missed weekends, all leading up to this major victory.

But instead of feeling elated, she seemed... hollow. She told me about the celebration dinner her firm had thrown for her the night before.

Her colleagues were clapping her on the back, telling her how brilliant she was. They raised their glasses in her honor. But as Pearl sat there, listening to them toast her success, she felt like a fraud. No matter how much praise she received, she couldn't shake the feeling that something was missing.

Then she told me about an encounter that really stuck with her. During the dinner, an old college friend named Rachel showed up. Pearl hadn't seen her in years, but they had been close during their time at law school.

Rachel looked genuinely happy—glowing even. As they caught up, Rachel mentioned her upcoming wedding and how excited she was to start a family.

She asked Pearl about her love life, but Pearl did what she always did: she brushed off the question with a joke about being married to her work. But deep down, it stung.

After the dinner, Pearl found herself standing outside in the cold Seattle night, staring at the lights of the city.

Rachel followed her out, and in that quiet moment, Pearl found herself admitting something she hadn't said out loud before. "I'm so tired," she told Rachel. "I'm tired of pretending that this is enough."

That was the turning point for Pearl. She realized that, for all her success, she had been shutting people out her entire life.

She had been too afraid to let anyone in, terrified that if they got too close, they'd see her for who she really was— someone who still felt unworthy of love, no matter how many cases she won or how high she climbed.

Over the next few months, we worked together to unpack that fear.

Pearl started to see that her emotional unavailability wasn't just affecting her relationships with others, but also her relationship with herself.

She had built these walls so high that even she couldn't see over them anymore.

When it comes to relationships, many women find themselves caught in patterns that seem impossible to break.

You might be fiercely independent in your career, have your life seemingly together, yet feel completely unravelled when it comes to love and intimacy.

You may wonder why you're so drawn to people who can't seem to meet you halfway, or why you constantly feel like you're walking on eggshells, terrified of being abandoned or not enough. If this sounds familiar, you're not alone.

This book is for women who want to understand why these patterns exist, and more importantly, how to break free from them. It's about healing the inner child that still carries the weight of unmet needs, fears, and insecurities.

Together, we'll explore where these feelings come from and how they manifest in your adult relationships, but most importantly, we'll focus on how you can cultivate a sense of security and worth within yourself, so that you no longer have to seek it from others.

Here is a simple Yes or No quiz to help you identify if you might have anxious attachment. Answer each question honestly based on your feelings and experiences in relationships:

Do you often worry that your partner or loved ones will leave you?
- *Yes*
- *No*

Do you frequently need reassurance from your partner or friends about their feelings for you?
- *Yes*
- *No*

Do you feel uneasy or anxious when your partner or loved ones are not immediately available to you (e.g., not responding to texts or calls)?
- *Yes*
- *No*

Do you tend to overanalyze your partner's words and actions, looking for signs they might be pulling away?

- *Yes*
- *No*

Do you feel like you are more invested in the relationship than your partner?

- *Yes*
- *No*

Do you fear being alone or feel a strong need to be in a relationship, even when it may not be healthy?

- *Yes*
- *No*

Do you often feel insecure about your worthiness in relationships?

- *Yes*
- *No*

When there is conflict or tension, do you become preoccupied with thoughts of the relationship ending?

- *Yes*
- *No*

Do you struggle to trust that your partner or loved ones genuinely care for you?

- *Yes*
- *No*

Do you feel intense anxiety when your partner expresses a need for space or independence?

- *Yes*
- *No*

Do you tend to blame yourself when things go wrong in relationships?

- *Yes*
- *No*

Scoring:

If you answered Yes to 6 or more of these questions, you might have anxious attachment tendencies. This is not a diagnosis but a starting point for understanding your attachment style and beginning the journey to more secure and fulfilling relationships.

> **_Our early attachment patterns affect our relationships, the way we love, and the way we connect with others for the rest of our lives. — Amir Levine, Attached_**

Chapter 1
Understanding Anxious Attachment

Lily was one of my most insightful clients. She came to me after what she described as the "perfect" relationship had unraveled right before her eyes. She had met Josh during her last year at the University of Texas in Austin.

They were both busy juggling demanding schedules—she was preparing for law school while he was finishing up a degree in engineering.

Despite the chaos, they found time for each other. From the very beginning, their connection felt intense and almost magnetic.

Josh had a quiet confidence that made Lily feel secure. He was attentive, kind, and everything she thought she wanted in a partner.

At first, everything was blissful. They spent every weekend together, exploring the city, finding hidden trails in the greenbelt, and sharing dreams about their future.

Josh would surprise her with thoughtful gestures—like bringing her coffee during her late-night study sessions or organizing small road trips to nearby towns when he knew she needed a break.

Lily couldn't believe how lucky she was. For the first time in her life, she felt like she was in a stable, loving relationship.

But underneath this perfect exterior, Lily was constantly battling a quiet storm. As much as Josh reassured her with his actions, her anxiety simmered beneath the surface.

She couldn't help but analyze every word he said, every text that took more than an hour to respond to, every slight change in his tone.

She'd lie awake at night wondering if Josh would get tired of her, if maybe he was just putting up with her because she was too much.

Lily hadn't shared these fears with him—she felt embarrassed by how needy she sounded, so she buried it deep inside, convincing herself she just needed to be more chill, more independent.

After about a year of dating, cracks began to show. Josh started working longer hours at his internship and spent less time with Lily.

He would still text and call, but the frequency began to dwindle. Lily's anxiety skyrocketed, but she didn't say anything.

She told herself she was being unreasonable, that Josh was just busy, and that her fears were irrational. She was terrified of pushing him away by voicing her concerns, so she bottled them up and pretended everything was fine.

One weekend, things came to a head. Josh had promised to spend Saturday with her after a particularly stressful week for both of them.

But on Friday night, he called to cancel—his boss had asked him to work on an urgent project, and he couldn't say no. Lily tried to act understanding on the phone, but the disappointment stung more than she wanted to admit. After hanging up, she felt that familiar knot of anxiety tighten in her chest.

She convinced herself that this was it—Josh was pulling away, and their relationship was falling apart.

The next day, Lily decided she couldn't take it anymore. She texted Josh, asking if they could talk. When they finally sat down together, she couldn't hold back her emotions.

She explained how scared she was of losing him, how she felt like he was growing distant, and how her anxiety had been eating her alive for months. She told him about all the sleepless nights, the obsessive thoughts, and the constant fear that he would leave her.

Josh listened quietly, his expression unreadable. When she was done, there was a long pause before he spoke. He told her he had noticed her pulling away too—trying to be "less needy"—but he had never understood why.

He admitted that her anxiety had been hard for him to handle because he didn't know how to help her.

But then, he said something that hit Lily like a punch to the gut: he wasn't sure if he could continue the relationship anymore.

He loved her, but he felt overwhelmed by the constant emotional pressure. He needed space to figure out what he wanted.

Lily's world shattered in that moment. Everything she had feared had come true. She felt like her worst nightmare was playing out in front of her eyes.

Josh, the man who had made her feel so safe and loved, was now telling her that she was too much to handle. She broke down, begging him to stay, to give their relationship another chance.

But Josh was firm. He needed time to think, and he wasn't sure if he could be the partner she needed.

The breakup wasn't immediate. They spent a few agonizing weeks in limbo, trying to see if they could make things work.

But ultimately, Josh decided to end it. Lily was devastated. She had built her entire future around him, and now that future was gone.

Months later, after our sessions had helped her piece together the emotional puzzle, Lily ran into Josh at a mutual friend's party.

They exchanged awkward pleasantries, and after a few drinks, they found themselves sitting on the porch, talking about the past. It was during that conversation that Josh admitted something Lily had never expected: he had his own emotional issues he had been hiding.

He had pulled away from her not because she was too much, but because he didn't feel worthy of her love. He had always struggled with his own fear of commitment and had been terrified of letting her down.

That revelation was a turning point for Lily. It didn't make everything better, but it gave her a new perspective. She realized that the end of their relationship wasn't entirely her fault, nor was it Josh's.

They had both been carrying emotional baggage they didn't know how to unpack at the time.

Have you ever caught yourself checking your phone repeatedly, anxiously waiting for a text to soothe your worries? Or maybe you've dissected every word your partner said, looking for hidden meanings or signs that they might be pulling away.

Perhaps you've even pushed people away in relationships, choosing to self-sabotage because the fear of being abandoned feels less terrifying than the vulnerability of being truly loved. If any of this feels familiar, you may be dealing with anxious attachment.

Anxious attachment isn't a flaw or a weakness; it's a survival strategy that our brains developed in response to early experiences of inconsistent or unpredictable love and attention.

As children, we learn to cling tightly to our caregivers, seeking their approval and affection. When those needs aren't reliably met, we grow up with a heightened sensitivity to rejection and abandonment.

This sensitivity often carries over into adulthood, affecting how we interact with partners, friends, and even coworkers.

Think of it like an overly sensitive smoke detector. Even the smallest hint of smoke sets off the alarm, blaring warnings when there's no real danger.

In a similar way, someone with anxious attachment has an emotional alarm system that's always on edge, reacting to the slightest perceived threat in their relationships.

This can show up in various ways, like constantly seeking reassurance, feeling jealous, or trying to control the situation.

The good news is that anxious attachment doesn't have to be permanent.

THE ROOTS OF ANXIOUS ATTACHMENT

Have you ever found yourself needing constant reassurance from your partner or feeling deeply uncomfortable at the thought of being alone?

Perhaps you've noticed a recurring pattern of choosing emotionally unavailable partners, only to end up in a cycle of heartache.

If this sounds familiar, you might be dealing with anxious attachment—a common issue that often stems from our earliest relationships.

To understand this better, think back to childhood. Imagine an infant who is entirely dependent on their caregivers, not just for physical needs like food and shelter, but also for emotional connection and security.

These early experiences shape our "internal working model," a psychological blueprint that influences how we perceive ourselves, others, and the world.

Attachment theory suggests that the quality of care we receive as infants plays a significant role in our ability to form secure relationships later in life.

When caregivers are consistently responsive and loving, the child develops a secure attachment style. They grow up trusting that their needs will be met and that they are deserving of love, which sets the foundation for healthy relationships in adulthood.

But life isn't always ideal. Some of us may have experienced caregivers who were inconsistent or emotionally unavailable, whether due to stress, distance, or other factors.

This inconsistent care can create insecurity and anxiety in a child, leading to what's known as an anxious attachment style.

Think of it like a plant that is watered irregularly—sometimes it gets what it needs, and other times it's left to wilt. This unpredictability causes the plant to struggle.

Similarly, a child who experiences inconsistent caregiving may grow up feeling anxious and unsure about when or if their emotional needs will be met. As adults, this can translate into seeking constant validation, clinging to others, and having difficulty trusting that relationships are stable.

Anxious attachment isn't a flaw or weakness; it's a response to early life experiences that shaped how we approach relationships. It's a protective mechanism that arises to guard against the perceived threats of abandonment or rejection.

IDENTIFYING ANXIOUS ATTACHMENT

Anxious attachment can feel like an emotional roller coaster, filled with ups and downs, doubts, and fears. Let's break down the emotions, thoughts, and behaviors associated with this attachment style to help you understand whether you or someone you know might be struggling with it.

Emotionally, those with anxious attachment often feel particularly vulnerable. They constantly seek reassurance, fearing that their loved ones will abandon them.

This fear can manifest as clinginess, excessive worry, or even panic when separated from their partners. It's similar to having an overly sensitive smoke alarm, constantly alerting them to threats that aren't truly there.

Jealousy is another common emotion. Individuals with anxious attachment may interpret any sign of interest their partner shows toward others as a threat, leading to suspicion, accusations, or attempts to control their partner's behavior. Every friendly interaction can feel like competition, feeding an endless loop of doubt.

Anxious attachment often comes with a set of negative thoughts and beliefs. People may see themselves as unlovable or flawed and often doubt the love and commitment of their partners.

It's like viewing the world through a distorted lens of insecurity, always on guard for signs of rejection. As a result, they may seek constant validation, whether through frequent communication, compliments, or extreme efforts to please their partners. No matter how much reassurance they get, it never feels like enough.

These patterns extend into behaviors as well. Common signs include clinginess, an overwhelming need for closeness, and anxiety when apart from their partner. People-pleasing is also common, where individuals sacrifice their own needs and desires to make others happy.

This behavior can leave them feeling drained and undervalued.

Trust issues may arise, even with partners who have shown reliability and love, leading to jealousy and suspicion.

Conflict avoidance is another common trait—often, they will sidestep difficult conversations or agree with their partner just to keep the peace, even if it means ignoring their own feelings.

In relationships, this attachment style can create an exhausting dynamic. The constant need for reassurance and fear of abandonment can cause misunderstandings and frequent arguments.

Partners may feel overwhelmed by the demands for attention and validation or frustrated by jealousy and controlling behaviors. Over time, this strain can lead to emotional withdrawal or even the end of the relationship.

E X E R C I S E

Create an "Attachment Timeline." Reflect on your early relationships with caregivers and write down key moments that shaped your understanding of love and security. Identify patterns of attachment behaviors that have influenced your relationships.

Steps:

Gather Materials:

- Get a piece of paper or journal and a pen. You can also use a digital document if you prefer.

Identify Early Caregivers:

- Think about the people who were responsible for your care during your early years. This could include parents, grandparents, or other caregivers.
- Write down their names and your relationship with each one.

Create a Timeline:

- Draw a horizontal line across your paper, representing your life from birth to your current age.
- Divide the timeline into different age ranges (e.g., 0-5, 6-10, 11-15, etc.).

Reflect on Key Moments:

- For each age range, think about specific memories or experiences with your caregivers. Focus on moments that shaped how you viewed love, safety, and relationships.
- Examples could include moments of affection, times you felt abandoned, or situations where you felt secure or anxious.
- Write these moments on the timeline at the appropriate age.

Identify Patterns:

- Look for patterns in your attachment experiences. For instance, did you often feel anxious when separated from a caregiver? Were there times when you felt consistently secure or cared for?
- Write these patterns down next to the corresponding experiences on your timeline.

Connect to Current Relationships:

- Reflect on how these early experiences have influenced your current relationships. Are there behaviors or fears you notice today that stem from those early patterns?
- Write down any connections or realizations you have about your attachment style and how it impacts your relationships.

Review and Reflect:

- Spend some time reviewing your timeline. Ask yourself how understanding these early patterns helps you better understand your attachment style and behavior in relationships today.

Use the template below or as a guide to create yours.

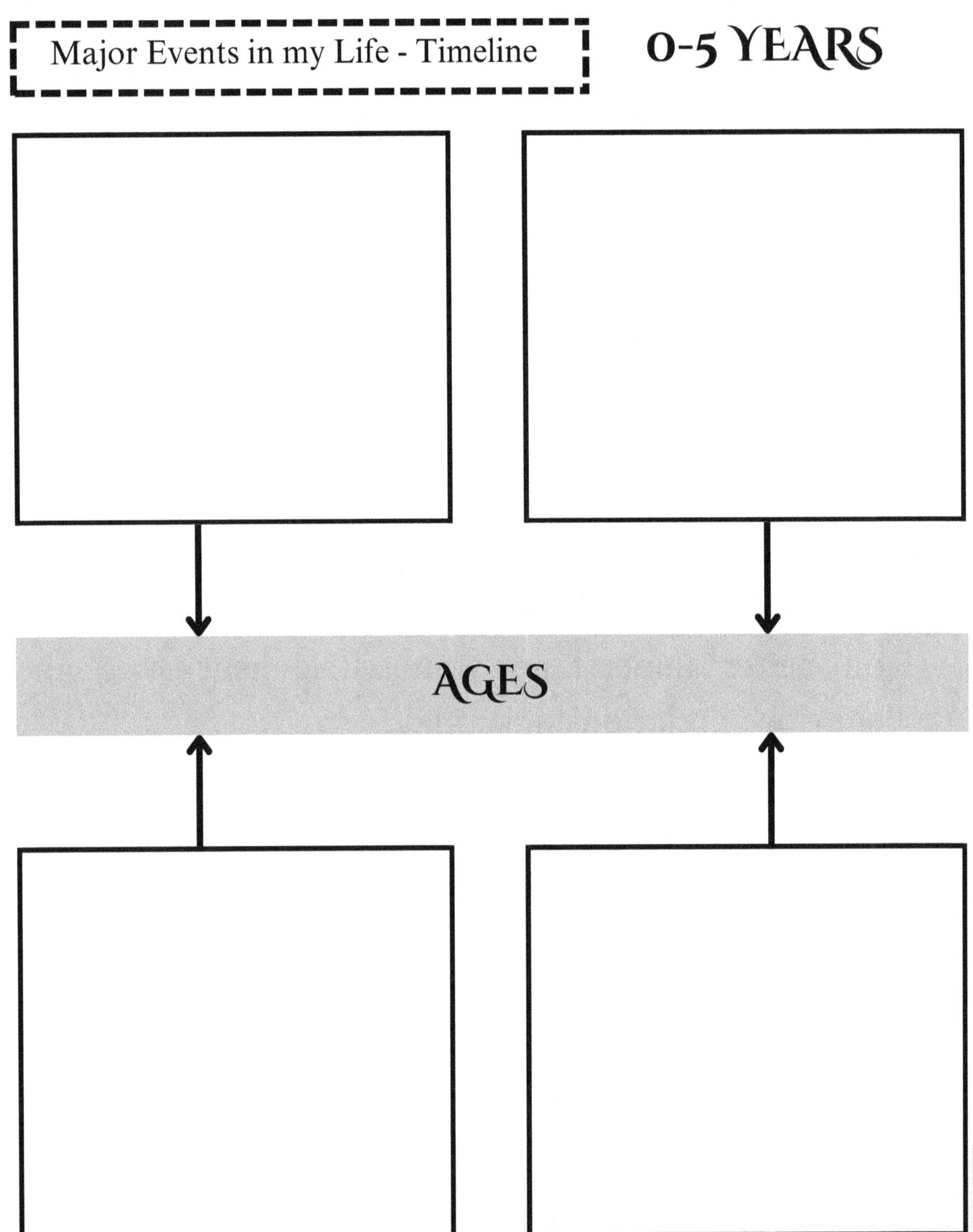
Major Events in my Life - Timeline
0-5 YEARS
AGES

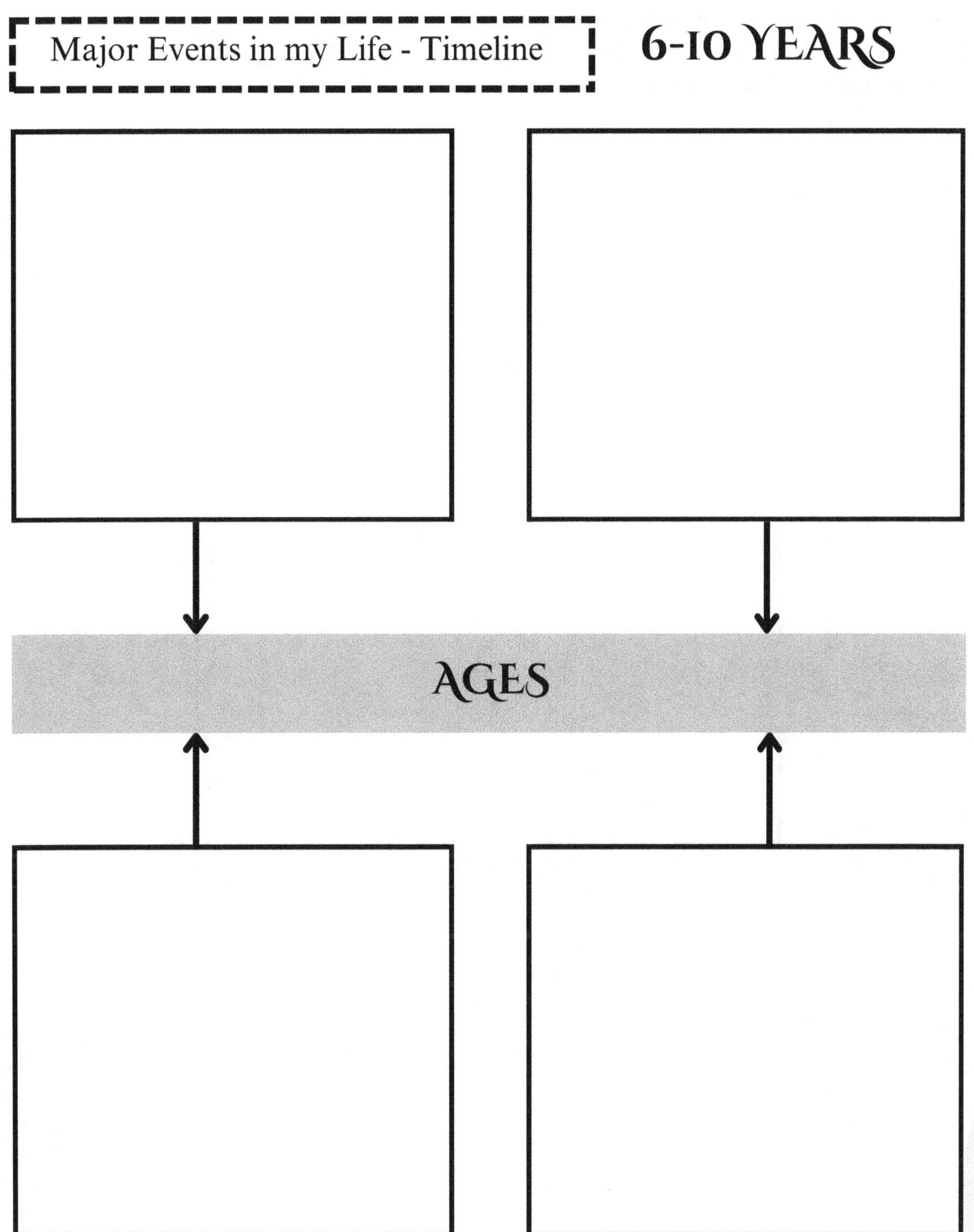
Major Events in my Life - Timeline
6-10 YEARS
AGES

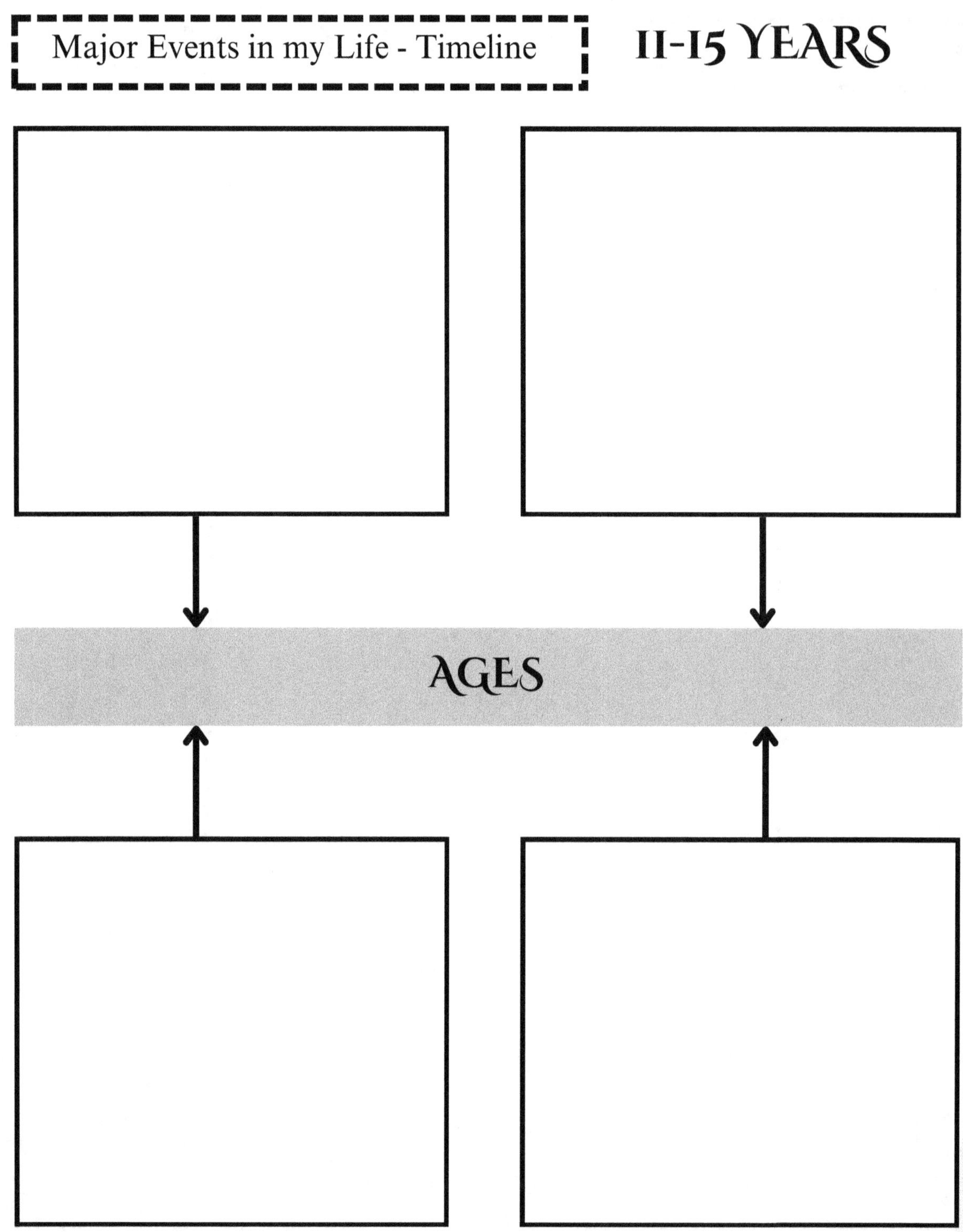

Major Events in my Life - Timeline
11-15 YEARS
AGES

Major Events in my Life - Timeline

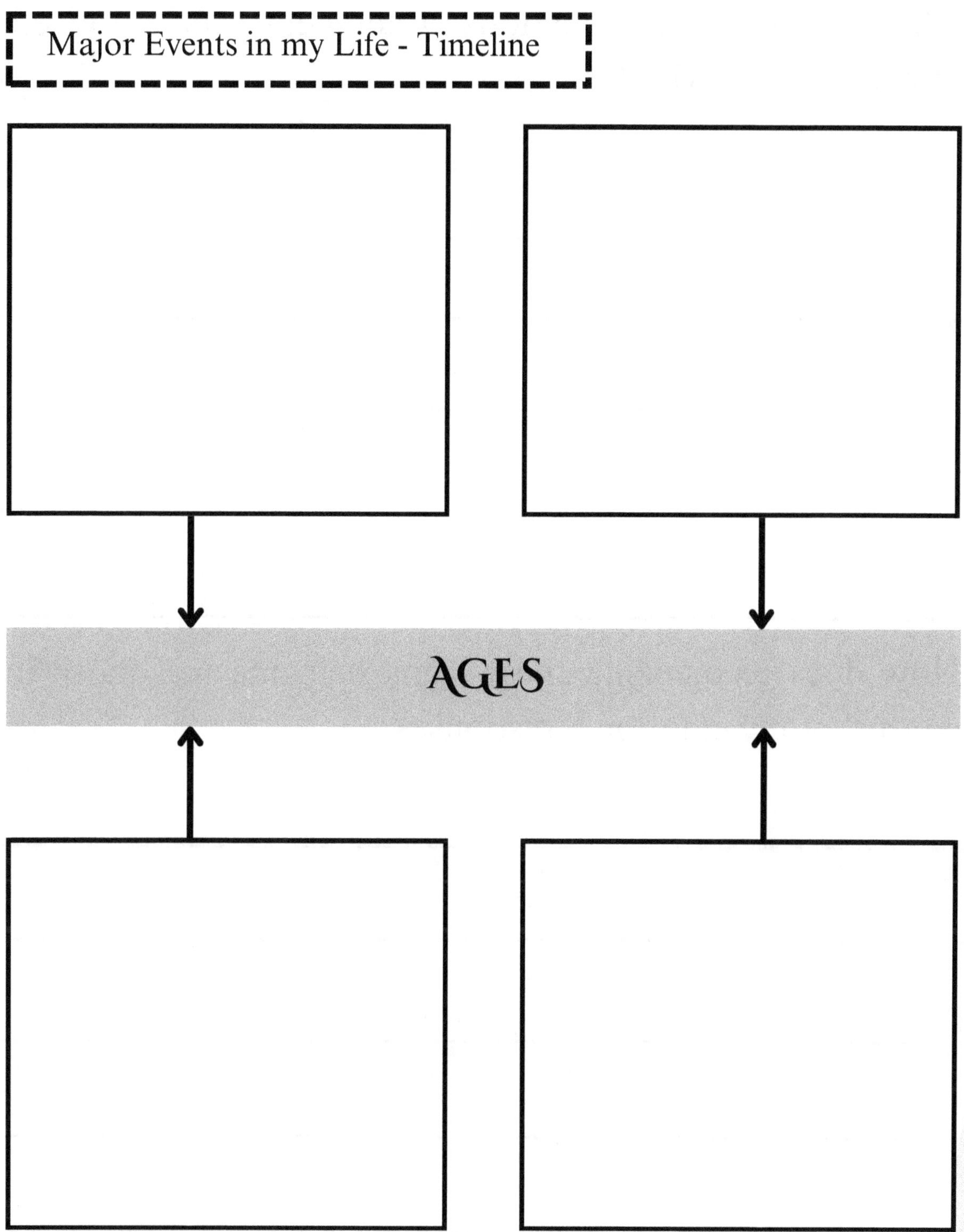

What are the signs of anxious attachment I have noticed in my own behavior?

____

____

____

____

How does recognizing these signs help me feel more in control of my emotional responses?

____

____

____

____

Chapter 2

THE INNER
CHILD'S WOUNDS

Ava sat across from me in the small, softly lit room, her hands resting on her lap, fingers twisting together nervously.

She was the type of person who never raised her voice, always calm, collected, and polite. If you met her in passing, you'd never suspect the storm that raged beneath her composed exterior.

Ava was the quintessential people pleaser—she kept everyone around her happy, even if it meant sacrificing her own needs.

But inside, Ava carried a silent rage that she had long buried, so deep that even she didn't recognize it until it started to surface in ways she couldn't control.

Ava grew up in a small town just outside of Austin, Texas. Her parents were pillars of the community—her father was the local pastor, and her mother ran charity events that brought the whole town together.

To everyone else, they seemed like the perfect family. But behind closed doors, the atmosphere was stifling. Her father ruled the household with a rigid, unspoken code of conduct. Emotions were seen as a weakness, something to be controlled and hidden.

Her mother, though kind and loving in her own way, was distant—never really present in the way Ava needed. She floated through life like a ghost, never showing anger, but never showing much affection either. Ava learned to mimic her mother's emotional distance while always seeking her approval, which never seemed to come.

Ava told me that her earliest memory of feeling anger was when she was about eight years old. Her younger brother had spilled juice on their mother's prized white carpet. Their mother had scolded them both harshly, her voice cold and detached.

But while her brother got away with a light slap on the wrist, Ava was forced to spend the entire afternoon scrubbing the stain, even though she hadn't caused it. She remembered how unfair it felt, the way her mother's disappointment lingered in the air, suffocating her. But she couldn't cry. She couldn't scream. She had to keep that perfect, polite mask on.

For years, Ava shoved her emotions deep down. In school, she was the model student, never causing trouble, always meeting expectations. She made friends easily, but those relationships were always superficial.

She never let anyone get too close. In romantic relationships, she repeated the same pattern—dating men who were emotionally unavailable, who mirrored her parents' distant and cold behavior.

She felt safe in those relationships because she never had to confront her own emotions.

Everything changed when she met Ryan. Ryan was kind, patient, and emotionally available in a way Ava had never experienced before.

He showered her with affection, listened to her every word, and made her feel like the center of his universe. At first, Ava thought she had finally found what she had been missing all her life.

But as the relationship deepened, something strange began to happen. Every time Ryan tried to get closer, Ava felt herself pulling away.

The intimacy made her feel exposed, vulnerable in a way she had never felt before, and with that vulnerability came a simmering anger she couldn't understand.

One day, it all came to a head. Ryan had suggested they move in together. It was a big step, one that any couple might celebrate. But instead of joy, Ava felt a wave of rage flood through her. She found herself yelling at Ryan, accusing him of trying to control her, of suffocating her.

She said things she didn't even mean, like how she never really loved him and how he was too needy for her. Ryan was stunned—this wasn't the woman he thought he knew.

Ava's anger shocked her too. Where had it come from? Why was she pushing away someone who truly loved her? That night, she cried herself to sleep, confused and ashamed. She had never felt so out of control before.

In therapy, as we explored Ava's past, we began to uncover the roots of her anger. Ava had never been allowed to express any negative emotions as a child.

She had learned to suppress her feelings, especially anger, because it was seen as dangerous or inappropriate in her family. But just because she suppressed those feelings didn't mean they went away. They were still there, buried deep inside her, waiting for a moment to erupt.

I guided Ava through exercises to connect with her inner child, that little girl who had felt powerless and silenced for so long.

Healing from anxious attachment involves an inner journey of reconnecting with the wounded child within.

This process requires acknowledging and validating the pain that child experienced, while offering the love and acceptance that was lacking during those formative years.

It also means building new, healthier coping mechanisms and relationship patterns that allow you to break free from the old cycles of insecurity and fear.

MEETING YOUR INNER CHILD

Remember the playground? The swing set soaring toward the sky, the merry-go-round spinning in a blur of laughter, the sandbox where castles rose and fell with the tide of imagination—that's where your inner child resides. Not in some far-off mystical place, but within you, a living memory of simpler times.

Your inner child isn't just a whimsical idea; it's a real, tangible part of you that experienced the world with wide-eyed wonder. It's the part of you that felt joy, sadness, fear, and anger with unfiltered intensity. And now, that child yearns to be seen, heard, and loved unconditionally.

You might be asking, "Why reconnect with my inner child? I'm an adult with responsibilities." But here's the truth: your inner child holds the key to understanding your anxious attachment patterns.

Reconnecting with this vulnerable part of yourself allows you to heal wounds from childhood, which transforms your adult relationships.

So, how do you begin this journey of reconnection? It starts with slowing down, quieting the outside noise, and turning your attention inward. You create a safe, non-judgmental space to meet your inner child and allow yourself to feel all the emotions that arise.

One powerful way to connect is through visualization. Find a quiet spot, close your eyes, and take a few deep breaths.

Picture yourself as a child, maybe at the playground or doing an activity you loved. Pay attention to the sights, sounds, and emotions you felt. Then, offer a hand to your younger self—tell them you see them, hear them, and love them.

You might even imagine embracing them, feeling the warmth of connection between you.

Journaling is another effective way to connect with your inner child. Write about your childhood experiences without worrying about structure. What memories come to mind? What emotions surface?

As you explore these memories, especially the painful ones, approach them with compassion. Remind yourself that your inner child was not responsible for what happened—they did the best they could.

Acknowledging your inner child's emotional experiences is a powerful step in healing. By saying, "I see you, I hear you, and I love you," you validate their feelings and begin to nurture the part of yourself that has been hurting for so long.

As you strengthen this connection, you'll start to notice shifts. Old patterns of anxious attachment might loosen their grip as you become more trusting, less reactive, and more confident in your worth. You may even rediscover the wonder and joy you once felt as a child.

Healing
The Past

While the causes of anxious attachment are complex, one undeniable truth stands out: childhood trauma and neglect can leave deep scars that echo into adulthood, profoundly shaping how we connect with others.

Let's be real—life isn't always full of sunshine and rainbows. We've all heard the saying, "What doesn't kill you makes you stronger," but sometimes what doesn't kill you can leave behind emotional baggage that affects everything from your self-esteem to your relationships.

Research suggests that about 70% of adults in the U.S. have faced some form of trauma during childhood. This statistic isn't exclusive to the U.S. either; trauma is a global issue that affects millions worldwide.

For those who've experienced childhood trauma or neglect, the world can often feel like a shaky, unsafe place. Maybe your parents were emotionally unavailable or unpredictable, leaving you feeling uncertain about their love.

Perhaps you witnessed violence or experienced abuse that shattered your sense of safety. Such experiences can plant the seeds of a deep fear of abandonment and a belief that you're unworthy of love or connection.

Childhood trauma affects our developing brains, shaping how we perceive the world and others. When trauma strikes early, our stress response systems can become overactive, making us more prone to anxiety and constantly on alert for danger.

We may carry negative beliefs about ourselves, viewing relationships through a lens of distrust and fear. Emotional regulation becomes a challenge, as overwhelming feelings of sadness, anger, or fear can surface seemingly without reason.

Neglect is one of the most common forms of childhood trauma. It isn't always about being denied physical needs; emotional neglect can be just as damaging.

When a child's emotional needs for love, attention, and validation aren't met, they may grow up feeling invisible and unimportant.

This sense of unworthiness can lead to anxious attachment in adulthood, where people cling to their partners out of fear of being abandoned. This constant need for reassurance and validation can strain even the strongest relationships.

Abuse—whether physical, emotional, or sexual—can also contribute to anxious attachment. Abuse shatters a child's trust and safety, making them feel powerless and afraid. In response, negative self-beliefs often form, such as "I am unlovable" or "I deserve to be hurt," which can sabotage future relationships.

However, it's important to remember that not everyone who experiences childhood trauma or neglect will develop anxious attachment.

Some people exhibit extraordinary resilience and form healthy, secure attachments despite facing adversity. But for many, the scars left by trauma affect their ability to form healthy connections.

If you resonate with these experiences, know that you're not alone, and healing is possible.

The first step is acknowledging how your childhood has influenced your current struggles. It's not an easy process —it can be painful to confront past wounds—but it's necessary for growth.

Professional therapy is often essential to trauma healing and developing secure attachment. A therapist can offer a safe space to process your past and work through your emotions.

They'll also guide you in building new, healthy relationship patterns and challenging the negative beliefs you've carried for so long.

Therapies like cognitive-behavioral therapy (CBT), eye movement desensitization and reprocessing (EMDR), and trauma-focused cognitive behavioral therapy (TF-CBT) have shown effectiveness in helping individuals recover from trauma.

Finding a therapist who specializes in trauma and has experience working with anxious attachment is key to making progress.

Beyond therapy, other resources can support your healing journey. Support groups provide a community of people who understand your struggles, offering empathy and encouragement.

Books, podcasts, and online resources can further your understanding and guide your healing. Practices like mindfulness, exercise, and spending time in nature can help reduce stress and foster emotional resilience.

Healing from anxious attachment is a gradual process that requires patience, support, and self-compassion. With time, you can break free from the patterns that no longer serve you and create relationships based on trust, security, and mutual respect.

EXERCISE

Write a letter to your inner child. In this letter, offer love, compassion, and understanding for the pain and confusion they experienced. Acknowledge the wounds from your past and begin to release them.

Step 1: Find a Quiet and Comfortable Space
- What to do: Choose a peaceful place where you won't be disturbed. Sit comfortably with a journal or a piece of paper and a pen.
- Why: This will help you focus and connect with your feelings without distractions.

Step 2: Close Your Eyes and Visualize Your Younger Self
- What to do: Close your eyes and imagine yourself as a child. Picture what you looked like at a younger age, perhaps during a time when you felt vulnerable or scared.
- Why: Visualizing your younger self can help you emotionally connect with that part of you, bringing empathy and compassion to the surface.

Step 3: Begin Your Letter with Love and Care

- What to do: Start your letter by addressing your inner child, perhaps using phrases like "Dear little [Your Name]," or simply "Dear Inner Child." Open with kind words, like you're speaking to a small, scared child.
- Example: "Dear little Isabella, I see how scared and confused you were back then, and I want you to know that I'm here for you now."
- Why: This sets a compassionate tone and allows your inner child to feel safe and understood.

Step 4: Acknowledge the Pain and Hurt

- What to do: Reflect on the difficult experiences your younger self went through. Acknowledge the emotions you felt, like fear, sadness, or loneliness. Let your inner child know that it's okay to feel those emotions.
- Example: "I know you felt abandoned when mom/dad wasn't there for you. It wasn't your fault, and you deserved to feel loved and protected."
- Why: Acknowledging past pain helps validate your inner child's feelings and begins the healing process.

Step 5: Offer Words of Comfort and Reassurance

- What to do: Offer comforting words to your inner child, reassuring them that things will be okay. Remind them that they are loved, valued, and no longer alone.
- Example: "You don't have to be scared anymore. I'm here now, and I will take care of you. You are strong, and you are worthy of love."
- Why: This reassures your inner child that they are safe now, which helps to soothe old wounds.

Step 6: Release the Past

- What to do: Gently encourage your inner child to let go of the pain from the past. Write about your commitment to protecting and nurturing them from now on, allowing them to release the hurt.
- Example: "I release the hurt and confusion from the past. We no longer need to carry this pain. I promise to protect and love you from now on."
- Why: Releasing the past helps you move forward and reduces the emotional burden your inner child has been holding onto.

Step 7: Close with Love and Encouragement

- What to do: End the letter with more love and kindness, affirming your commitment to healing and embracing your inner child moving forward.
- Example: "You are loved. You are safe. Together, we will heal and grow."
- Why: Closing with love reinforces the positive message and creates a sense of closure and empowerment.

Step 8: Reflect and Keep the Letter

- What to do: Take a moment to reflect on how you feel after writing the letter. You can choose to keep the letter in a safe place, reread it when you need reassurance, or even write new letters as you continue healing.
- Why: This reflection allows you to acknowledge your progress and see the letter as a tool for ongoing healing.

How does reconnecting with my inner child make me feel?

____

____

____

____

What past experiences have I been carrying that still impact my relationships today?

____

____

____

____

The greatest gift you can give someone is the space to be his or herself, without the threat of you leaving.— Kai Greene

Chapter 3
BUILDING A SECURE BASE WITHIN

Rebecca came to me at a time when she was ready to give up on her marriage. She was a 38-year-old mother of two, living in Austin, Texas, with her husband of 12 years. From the outside, everything seemed perfect.

They had a beautiful home in the suburbs, their kids were thriving in school, and her husband, Mark, was the type of man that other women would envy: supportive, loving, and always there for her. But beneath the surface, Rebecca was drowning in anxiety.

She confided in me during one of our first sessions, "I feel like he's going to leave me. I don't know why, but I'm just waiting for it to happen." Her voice shook, and she was twisting her wedding ring absentmindedly, something she did whenever her nerves took over.

It didn't make sense to her; Mark hadn't done anything wrong. In fact, he tried his best to reassure her. But no matter how much he loved her, she couldn't shake the feeling that it wasn't enough.

Rebecca's anxiety was constant. She would text Mark multiple times during the day, and if he didn't respond quickly, she'd immediately assume the worst.

If he had a long day at work and wasn't as affectionate when he came home, her mind would spiral into thoughts of abandonment.

She admitted to checking his phone when he wasn't around, even though she hated herself for it. It wasn't rational, but that was how deeply ingrained her fear of being left was.

As we peeled back the layers of her story, it became clear that her childhood was the source of this deep-rooted insecurity. Growing up, her parents had a chaotic relationship. Her father was a quiet man, always busy with work and rarely present.

He was emotionally unavailable, not because he didn't care, but because he didn't know how to connect. Her mother, on the other hand, was unpredictable. Some days she would shower Rebecca with affection, almost smothering her with love. Other days, she would withdraw completely, leaving Rebecca to wonder what she had done wrong.

That inconsistency left Rebecca with a wound she had carried into her marriage. She learned early on that love was not something you could count on.

It was something you had to fight for, cling to, and protect at all costs. As a result, she had developed a pattern of testing Mark's love, of always needing to be reassured that he wasn't going anywhere.

But the more she clung, the more distant Mark became. She described the tension in their home as suffocating.

Mark would try to help by giving her space, thinking it would calm her, but it only made things worse. She felt like he was pulling away, and in her mind, that was a clear sign that her worst fear was coming true.

One evening, after another argument where she accused him of not caring enough, Mark broke down. He told her he couldn't keep living like this.

He loved her, but the constant pressure to prove it was wearing him down. Rebecca was devastated. She knew he was right, but she didn't know how to stop. That's when she decided to come to therapy.

As we worked together, I helped Rebecca start to understand where her anxiety was coming from. We talked about her parents, how their inconsistent love had shaped her understanding of relationships.

I introduced her to the concept of self-compassion, which was something she had never considered before. Rebecca had spent her whole life looking for security outside of herself, but I wanted her to start finding it within.

At first, it was difficult. She had always been so focused on making sure everyone around her was okay that she had never taken the time to care for herself. I encouraged her to start small.

When she felt the familiar pang of anxiety that Mark was pulling away, instead of immediately reacting by seeking reassurance, she would pause and try to soothe herself.

We worked on emotional regulation techniques, like deep breathing and grounding exercises, to help her stay calm in those moments of fear.

As you cultivate self-compassion and emotional regulation, a profound transformation will take place within you. You'll begin to notice that your relationship with yourself becomes healthier and more supportive.

You'll feel more grounded, centered, and confident in your ability to handle whatever life throws your way. This sense of inner strength will naturally extend to your relationships with others.

With a secure foundation within yourself, you'll find that you no longer need constant validation from external sources.

You'll be more comfortable setting healthy boundaries and communicating your needs openly and effectively. You'll trust that even when things don't go as planned, you will be okay because your self-worth isn't tied to outside approval or outcomes.

This doesn't mean that insecurity or fear will never surface again. But now, you'll have the tools to navigate those emotions with grace and resilience, without letting them undermine your sense of worth. By building this inner stability, you'll create healthier, more fulfilling relationships, based on mutual respect and genuine connection.

CULTIVATING SELF-COMPASSION

Nova sat across from me, tension radiating from her like heat from a furnace. The industrial atmosphere of the manufacturing plant where she worked was worlds away from the comfort of my therapy office, but her anxieties were all too familiar: an unrelenting fear of abandonment, a deep-rooted belief that she wasn't enough, and a history of failed relationships to prove it.

Like many of my clients, Nova was tangled in the painful grasp of anxious attachment. Her inner critic was merciless, constantly feeding her doubts and insecurities. Though she longed for love and connection, her fear of rejection led her to cling to her partners, ultimately driving them away.

It was evident that Nova needed to embark on a journey of self-compassion—something as foreign to her as a tropical beach is to a penguin.

Self-compassion isn't about indulging yourself or turning a blind eye to your flaws.

It's about treating yourself with the same kindness and understanding you'd offer a close friend. It's recognizing your humanity, and like all humans, understanding that you're imperfect.

Mindfulness is a powerful way to foster self-compassion. It involves being present in the moment without judgment. When those self-critical thoughts begin to surface, gently acknowledge them, then bring your focus back to your breath or your surroundings.

Think of your inner critic as a cranky old parrot perched on your shoulder. You don't have to believe every squawk it makes. Instead, thank it for its opinion, and then calmly ask it to quiet down while you focus on more positive, helpful thoughts.

A key component of self-compassion is challenging negative self-talk. The voice in your head that says, "You're not good enough" or "You'll never be loved" isn't speaking the truth. It's a distorted view driven by your anxious attachment.

When you catch yourself engaging in negative self-talk, pause and ask, "Would I say this to a friend?" If the answer is no, then why say it to yourself? Reframe those negative thoughts into more compassionate, realistic ones. Instead of "I'm a failure," try "I'm learning and growing."

Embracing imperfection is another cornerstone of self-compassion. Everyone has flaws, quirks, and vulnerabilities—it's what makes us human. Striving for perfection is exhausting and impossible. Instead, focus on accepting yourself as you are, imperfections and all.

Picture yourself as a beautifully flawed piece of pottery. You might have chips or cracks, but they don't diminish your worth or your capacity to hold something precious. In fact, those imperfections add to your character.

Remember, self-compassion isn't a one-time fix; it's an ongoing practice. Some days will be easier than others.

There will be moments when your inner critic is particularly loud and relentless. But with patience and persistence, you can learn to quiet that voice and build a more compassionate relationship with yourself.

Nova, my client with anxious attachment, slowly began to embrace self-compassion. It wasn't easy. She faced setbacks and moments of doubt. But she persevered, and as she did, her relationship with herself started to change.

She learned to challenge her negative self-talk, replacing those harsh criticisms with words of support and understanding. She practiced mindfulness, grounding herself in the present and silencing the anxieties that once consumed her. She embraced her imperfections, understanding that they did not define her.

As Nova's self-compassion grew, her relationships improved as well. No longer driven by fear of abandonment, she was able to connect with others in a more genuine and meaningful way. She even started dating again, this time with a newfound sense of self-worth and confidence.

EMOTIONAL REGULATION

Anxious attachment often feels like you're constantly on edge, living in a state of heightened alertness. It's that persistent hum of anxiety, the gnawing sensation in your gut that something is about to go wrong.

When your partner doesn't reply to a text right away, it's not just a small frustration—it feels like a sign they're pulling away.

When a friend cancels plans, it's not just disappointing—it feels like a personal rejection. You may catch yourself dissecting every word, every look, every slight change in tone, convinced there's a hidden meaning you're missing.

And that's just the beginning. Anxious attachment can trigger a whole host of physical symptoms. Your heart might race, your palms might sweat, your breathing might become shallow and rapid. You might struggle with sleeping, focusing, or even just relaxing. It's as if your body has become hyper-attuned to sensing danger, even when none exists.

So, how do you cope when fear and anxiety start taking over? Start by taking a deep breath. And then another. And another. It may sound simple, but deep breathing exercises can do wonders for calming your nervous system. It's like pressing the pause button on your stress response.

Think of your breath as your anchor. When your mind is racing and emotions are swirling, your breath remains steady and constant. By focusing on it, you can ground yourself in the present moment, easing the internal chaos.

But what if deep breathing doesn't fully calm your anxiety? That's where grounding techniques come into play. These methods help you reconnect with your body and surroundings, pulling you away from the spiral of anxious thoughts.

A straightforward grounding exercise is the 5-4-3-2-1 method. Begin by identifying five things you can see, four things you can touch, three things you can hear, two things you can smell, and one thing you can taste.

This exercise engages your senses, anchoring you in the present and drawing you away from the "what-ifs" and worst-case scenarios that anxious attachment thrives on.

Next, let's talk about cognitive reframing. This technique involves changing how you interpret situations. Anxious attachment often leads to catastrophizing—imagining the worst-case scenario. Cognitive reframing helps you challenge these negative assumptions and replace them with more balanced, realistic ones.

For example, if your partner is running late, instead of immediately assuming they're upset with you or pulling away, try considering other explanations. Maybe they're stuck in traffic or delayed by work. Maybe they just lost track of time. By questioning your initial thoughts, you take the power away from anxiety and prevent it from spiraling.

Managing anxiety and fear is not easy—it takes effort, patience, and a lot of self-kindness. But with the right tools and support, you can start quicting the alarm bells of anxious attachment and create a life that feels calmer and more fulfilling.

E X E R C I S E

Practice self-compassion by engaging in a "Loving-Kindness Meditation." Focus on sending love and kindness to yourself, acknowledging your worth, and reminding yourself that you are deserving of love and care.

Step 1: Find a Quiet, Comfortable Space
Sit in a comfortable position in a quiet space where you won't be disturbed. You can close your eyes or keep them slightly open with a soft gaze.

Step 2: Focus on Your Breathing
Take a few deep breaths in and out. Allow your body to relax with each exhale. Focus on your breath, letting it flow naturally without forcing it.

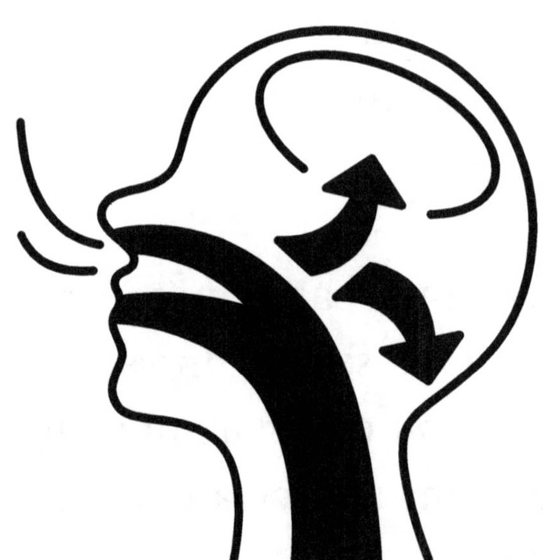

Step 3: Begin with Self-Compassion

Start by silently repeating gentle phrases of love and kindness to yourself. You can use phrases like:

"May I be happy."

"May I be healthy."

"May I be safe."

"May I live with ease."

Say each phrase slowly and with intention. Let the meaning of the words sink in.

Step 4: Visualize Yourself with Love

As you say these phrases, imagine yourself surrounded by warmth and love. Picture yourself receiving the kindness and care you are sending. You might even place a hand on your heart to reinforce the feeling of compassion.

Step 5: Acknowledge Your Worth

Remind yourself that you are deserving of love, just as you are. Think about moments when you've been hard on yourself, and replace those feelings with understanding and kindness.

Step 6: Continue for 5-10 Minutes

Continue repeating these phrases and focusing on sending yourself love for about 5-10 minutes. If your mind wanders, gently bring your attention back to the phrases and your breathing.

Step 7: Gradually End the Meditation

When you feel ready, slowly bring your awareness back to the present moment. Take a few deep breaths, open your eyes (if they were closed), and take a moment to notice how you feel.

Step 8: Carry the Compassion with You

As you go about your day, try to carry the sense of compassion and kindness with you. Remember that you are deserving of love and care at all times.

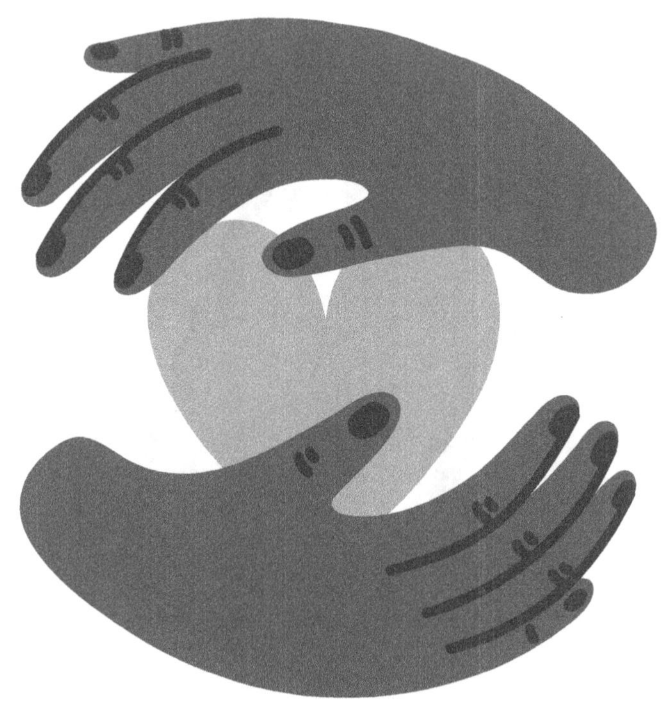

How do I typically respond to myself when I am feeling anxious or afraid?

____

____

____

____

What makes self-compassion difficult for me, and how can I overcome that?

____

____

____

____

What we have is an attachment to someone, often based on fears of abandonment or emotional wounds, rather than true love.
— David Richo

Chapter 4

REWRITING YOUR RELATIONSHIP PATTERNS

Laura and Emma were best friends throughout high school in Portland, Oregon. Their bond was formed over shared classes, late-night study sessions, and the thrill of teenage adventures.

Laura, a vibrant and warm-hearted individual, had always been the life of their group. Emma, on the other hand, was more reserved, content to listen and support her friends from the sidelines.

Their friendship was put to the test when Laura's younger brother, Jake, tragically died in a car accident during their senior year. The loss hit Laura like a tidal wave. The grief left her feeling abandoned and emotionally adrift. She began to cling to Emma more intensely, seeking constant reassurance that she wasn't alone.

Emma, who was struggling to manage her own stress from college applications and family expectations, found it increasingly difficult to keep up with Laura's heightened needs.

Emma hoped that taking a small step back would give Laura space to begin processing her grief and find some independence. She hoped Laura would slowly start to rely on a broader support network, rather than depending solely on her.

However, Laura misinterpreted Emma's distance as a sign of abandonment. She felt that Emma, her closest friend, was withdrawing from her just when she needed her most.

Secure relationships form the foundation of a fulfilling life. When we feel safe and cherished, we're more resilient, confident, and equipped to handle life's challenges.

Yet, for those dealing with anxious attachment, building and maintaining healthy connections can seem like a constant struggle. But it doesn't have to be this way.

Imagine a life where your relationships are a source of joy, support, and personal growth, rather than anxiety and fear. Picture feeling secure in your partner's love and confident in your self-worth. This vision isn't just a fantasy; it's an achievable goal. The key is to recognize and change your relationship patterns.

Anxious attachment often leads us to unconsciously replicate the dynamics of our early relationships, even if those dynamics were unhealthy or painful.

We might find ourselves constantly seeking reassurance, fearing abandonment, or grappling with jealousy and insecurity. These behaviors can undermine even the most promising relationships, leaving us feeling drained and unsatisfied.

The good news is that you can break free from these damaging patterns. By understanding the origins of your anxious attachment and adopting new ways of relating to others, you can transform your relationships and cultivate a more secure and fulfilling love life.

The path to healing these wounds is not always smooth, but it is achievable. It demands patience, self-compassion, and a readiness to confront difficult emotions. However, the rewards are profound. As you heal your inner child and learn to embrace and love yourself, you'll notice positive changes in your relationships.

You'll begin to feel more secure in your partner's affection and less fearful of abandonment. You'll communicate your needs more effectively and establish healthier boundaries. You'll also develop a deeper trust in yourself and others.

Rewriting your relationship patterns is not about becoming someone else. It's about uncovering your true self beneath the layers of fear and insecurity. It's about reclaiming your power and crafting the love life you deserve.

HEALTHY COMMUNICATION

Communicating our needs and setting boundaries can feel like walking a tightrope, especially for those dealing with anxious attachment.

The fear of rejection or abandonment often leaves us silenced, with unmet needs and overstepped boundaries. Yet, mastering this skill is essential for building healthy relationships and reclaiming our personal power.

Think of it like learning a new dance—awkward at first, but with practice, it becomes second nature.

Let's begin with expressing your needs. It's not about becoming demanding, but about clearly stating what you need to feel safe, loved, and respected.

Imagine giving your partner a treasure map to your heart's desires. Instead of saying, "You never listen to me," try, "I feel ignored when I talk about my day. Could you please put your phone away and give me your full attention?"

he latter approach focuses on your feelings and makes a specific request, making it easier for your partner to respond constructively.

Now, let's address boundaries. If your personal space feels like a public park, it's time to set some boundaries. Boundaries aren't about building walls; they're about creating a safe space where you can thrive.

They let others know how you want to be treated, what you'll tolerate, and what's off-limits. This might seem intimidating, but remember, you're the architect of your life. You decide who gets a front-row seat and who's in the nosebleed section.

Setting boundaries involves assertiveness—a skill many of us need to develop. It's about standing up for yourself without being aggressive.

Think of it as the Goldilocks principle—not too passive, not too aggressive, but just right. "No" is a complete sentence, and you don't need to justify your decisions.

Conflict is an inevitable part of relationships. It's not about avoiding disagreements, but about how you handle them.

When conflict arises, resist the urge to shut down or lash out. Instead, take a deep breath and try to understand your partner's perspective. Remember, you're on the same team, working towards a healthy, fulfilling relationship.

Effective communication, healthy boundaries, and constructive conflict resolution are not just buzzwords— they're the cornerstones of lasting love. It's not about being perfect; it's about making progress.

Even small steps toward healthier communication can create a positive ripple effect in your relationships. You're not alone in this journey.

Many resources, including therapists, support groups, and self-help books, are available to support you. Don't hesitate to seek help if you need it.

Consider this scenario: Your partner often checks their phone during dinner, making you feel unimportant.

Instead of stewing in silence, you could say, "I really value our time together, and it makes me feel disconnected when you're on your phone. Could you put it away during dinner?" This approach is assertive yet respectful, focusing on your feelings and desired outcome.

It opens the door for a healthy conversation and potential behavior change.

Or perhaps you have a friend who frequently vents about their problems, leaving you feeling drained. Instead of withdrawing, you might set a boundary by saying, "I care about you, but I also need to protect my own energy. I'm happy to listen for a bit, but let's switch to a different topic after that." This way, you honor both your needs and the friendship.

Remember, this is a marathon, not a sprint. Developing healthy communication patterns takes time and effort, especially when overcoming anxious attachment. Be patient with yourself, celebrate your small victories, and don't be afraid to ask for help when needed.

OVERCOMING JEALOUSY AND INSECURITY

Jealousy and insecurity can feel like constant, unwelcome companions, especially if you have anxious attachment. It's like a nagging feeling when your partner chats a little too long with a barista or takes their time responding to a text.

These feelings often come from a deep fear of abandonment. It's as if there's a persistent voice telling you that you're not good enough and that your partner will leave you.

This fear can make small things seem like major threats, turning an innocent interaction into a potential affair or a missed text into a sign of disinterest.

However, you don't have to let these fears control your life. It's possible to break free from this cycle and build trust and security in your relationships. Start by being kind to yourself.

Instead of criticizing yourself for feeling insecure, treat yourself with compassion and recognize that these feelings are rooted in past experiences, not your value.

Building trust in yourself is also important. This means learning to rely on your own judgment and intuition rather than constantly seeking reassurance from others. It involves setting boundaries, clearly expressing what you need, and taking responsibility for your own happiness.

Open communication with your partner is crucial. Share your fears and feelings in a way that encourages understanding rather than blame. For instance, instead of accusing your partner of flirting with others, explain that their behavior makes you feel insecure and anxious. This way, you invite a constructive conversation about your feelings.

Trust takes time and effort to develop. It's like tending to a delicate plant; it needs care and patience from both partners. Celebrate the progress you make together and remember that trust is built through consistent actions, open communication, and respect.

It's also important to understand that trust is mutual. Just as you need to trust your partner, they need to trust you.

This means being reliable, keeping promises, and respecting each other's boundaries. Honesty and transparency are key.

If trust has been broken, it's essential to assess the situation carefully. Minor issues might be resolved with open dialogue and effort, but serious betrayals may need professional help to address. Take the time to deal with these issues thoughtfully and seek support if necessary.

Ultimately, dealing with jealousy and insecurity is a process. With self-compassion, effective communication, and time, you can create stronger, more secure relationships and build deeper trust in yourself and others.

EXERCISE

Create a "Boundaries Map." List current relationships and note where boundaries need to be set or reinforced. Then, practice communicating one of these boundaries with someone in a safe and supportive environment.

Step 1: List Your Relationships

- Grab a Notebook or Document: Start with a notebook, a blank sheet of paper, or a digital document.
- Write Down Names: List all the people in your life with whom you have ongoing relationships. This might include family members, friends, colleagues, and significant others.

Step 2: Identify Boundary Needs

- Reflect on Each Relationship: For each person listed, think about where you feel your boundaries might be lacking or need reinforcement.

- Note Boundary Areas: Next to each name, jot down specific areas where boundaries are needed. This could include issues like personal space, time management, emotional support, or respect for privacy.

Step 3: Categorize Boundaries

- Group Similar Boundaries: Look at your list and see if there are common themes or categories. For instance, you might find that several relationships need boundaries around personal time or communication styles.
- Prioritize Boundaries: Decide which boundaries are most important to address first. Start with the relationships where boundary-setting will have the most significant positive impact.

Step 4: Plan How to Communicate Boundaries

- Choose a Boundary to Start With: Pick one boundary from your list that you want to focus on first. Consider choosing a boundary that feels achievable and where you feel relatively confident.

- Plan Your Approach: Think about how you want to communicate this boundary. Write down or mentally outline what you want to say, making sure to be clear, direct, and respectful.

Step 5: Practice in a Safe Environment

- Role-Play the Conversation: Find a supportive friend or family member who can help you practice setting this boundary. Share your planned approach with them and rehearse the conversation.
- Seek Feedback: After role-playing, ask for feedback on how you communicated the boundary. This can help you refine your approach and build confidence.

Step 6: Communicate the Boundary

- Choose the Right Time and Setting: Once you feel prepared, find a suitable time to talk to the person about your boundary. Ensure it's a calm and private setting where both of you can focus on the conversation.
- Be Clear and Respectful: Communicate your boundary clearly and respectfully. Use "I" statements (e.g., "I need to have some quiet time in the evenings") to express your needs without blaming or accusing.

Step 7: Reflect and Adjust

- Review the Outcome: After the conversation, reflect on how it went. Consider how the other person responded and how you felt during and after the discussion.
- Adjust if Needed: If the boundary wasn't respected or if the conversation didn't go as planned, adjust your approach as needed and try again. Boundaries are a process and may need ongoing adjustments.

Use the template below as a guide

Boundaries Map

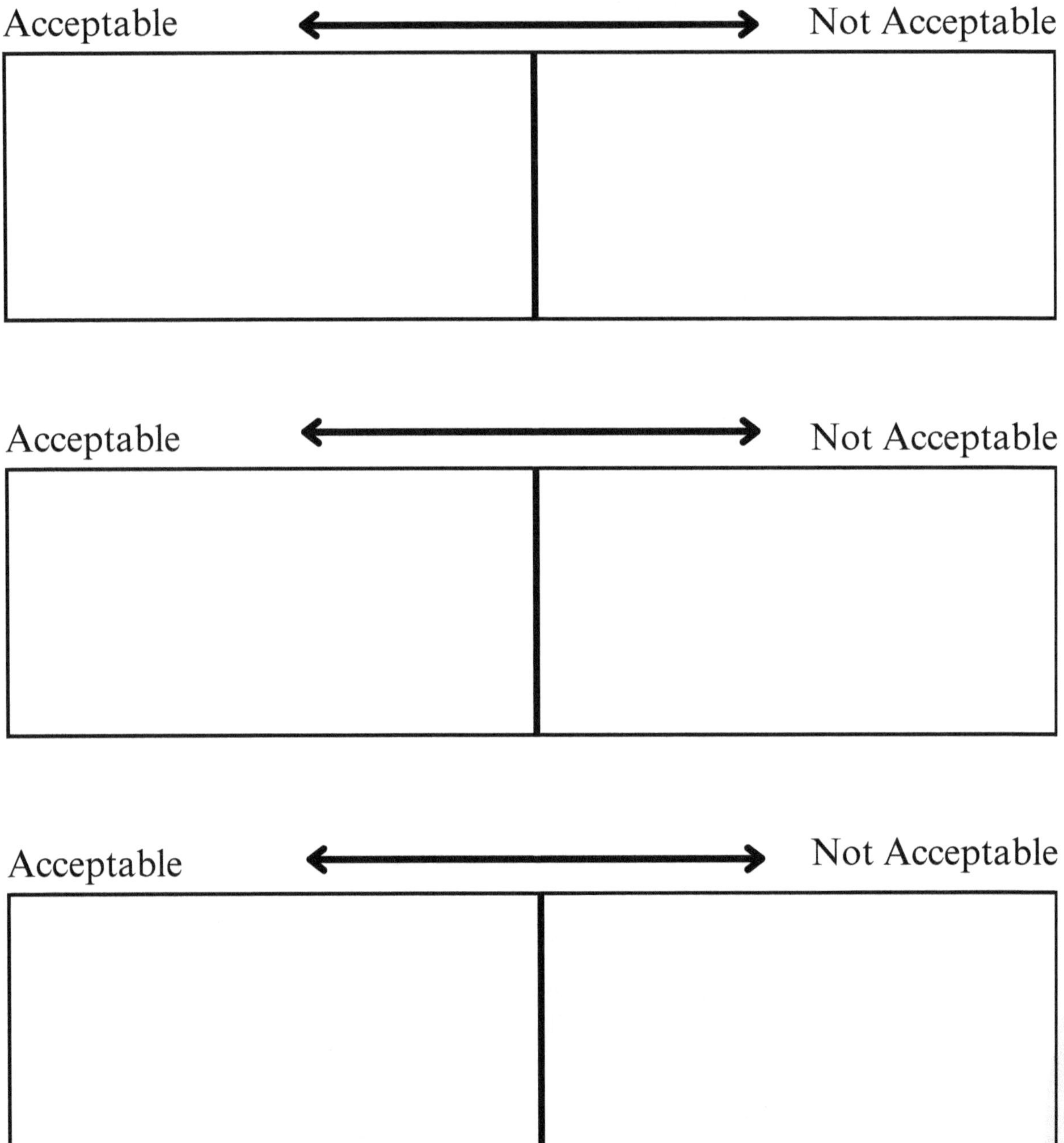

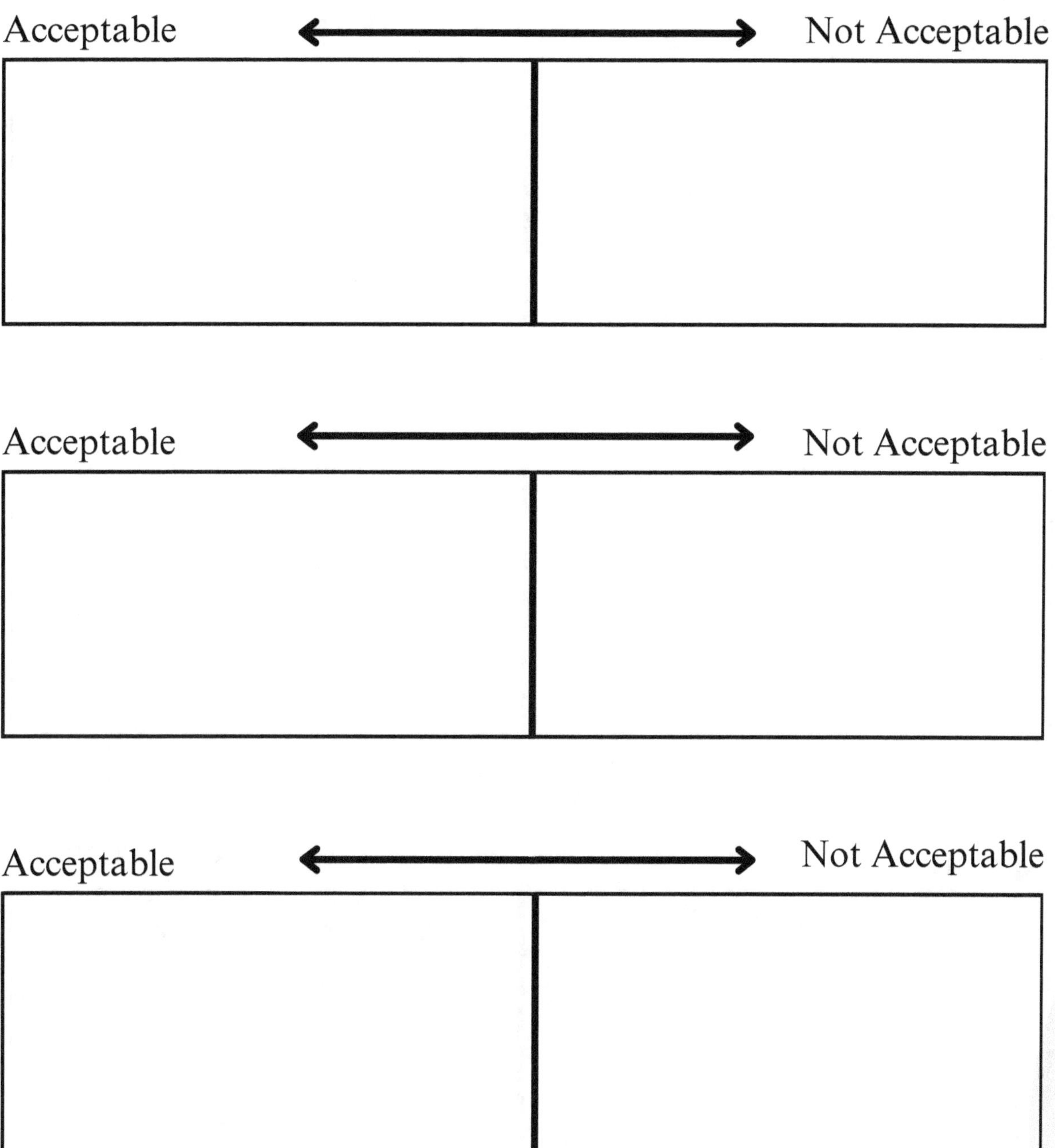

Acceptable
Not Acceptable
Acceptable
Not Acceptable
Acceptable
Not Acceptable

Acceptable   ⟷   Not Acceptable

Acceptable   ⟷   Not Acceptable

Acceptable   ⟷   Not Acceptable

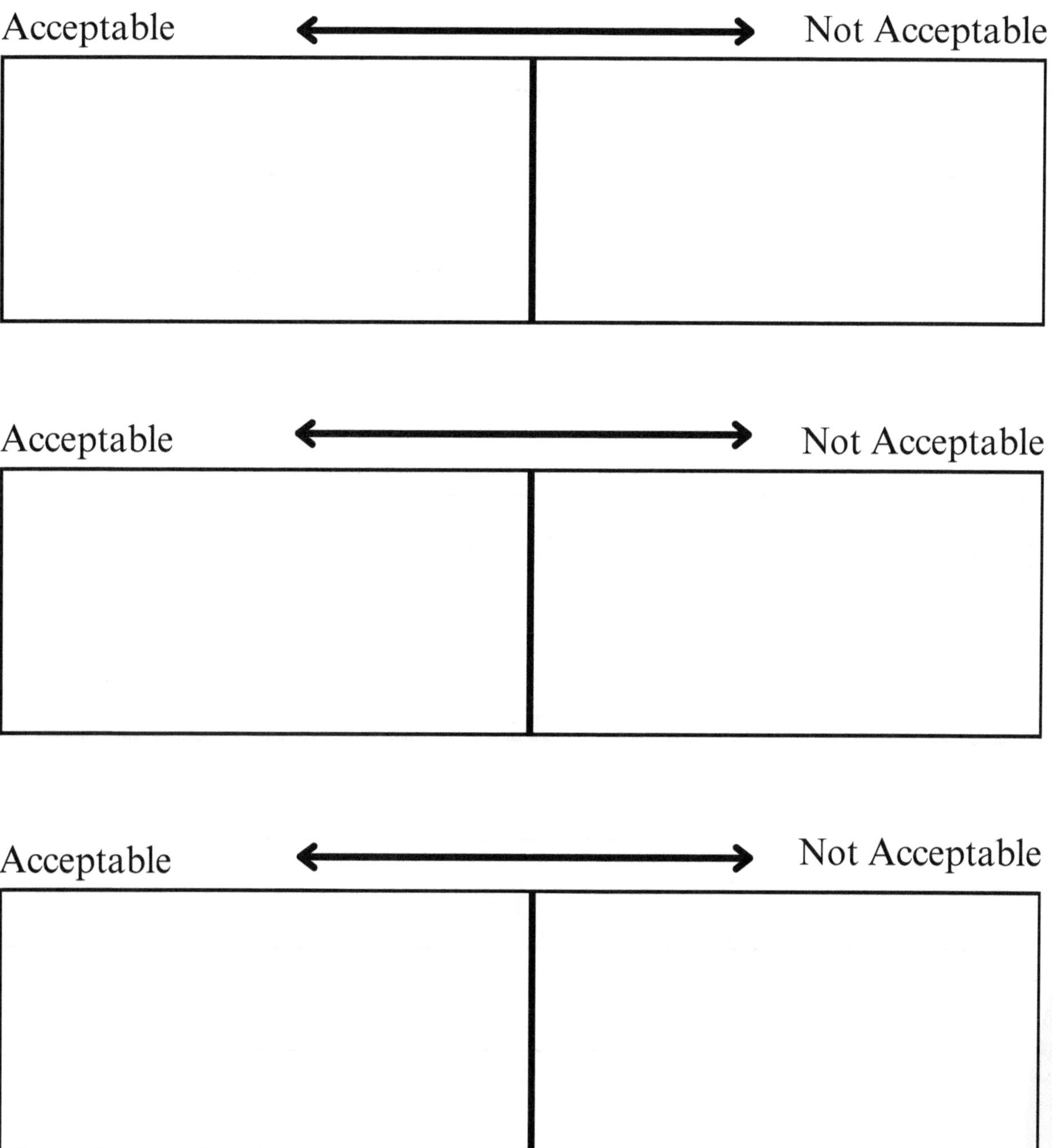
Acceptable
Not Acceptable
Acceptable
Not Acceptable
Acceptable
Not Acceptable

How do I express my needs in relationships, and what fears arise when I do?

____

____

____

____

How has jealousy and insecurity impacted my relationships in the past?

____

____

____

____

Chapter 5

CULTIVATING SELF-WORTH

Maria grew up in a bustling suburb of Dallas, Texas, with a mother who was incredibly protective and overly accommodating.

Her mother, Janet, had her own anxieties and insecurities, which she channeled into being excessively attentive to Maria's every need.

From the moment Maria was born, Janet's world revolved around ensuring her daughter's safety and happiness, often at the expense of her own well-being.

Janet would hover over Maria, managing every aspect of her life from school projects to social interactions. She was always there, making decisions for Maria and stepping in to fix any problems before Maria even had a chance to learn how to handle them on her own.

This overprotective behavior, although rooted in love, left Maria feeling like she was incapable of managing her own life. Janet's anxieties about Maria's future created an environment where Maria was not given the chance to develop independence or self-reliance.

As Maria grew older, this dynamic began to take its toll. Despite excelling academically and being a model student, Maria felt paralyzed by self-doubt.

She often questioned whether her achievements were genuinely her own or just the result of her mother's interventions.

The constant need for reassurance from others became a coping mechanism. She found herself anxiously seeking validation in every aspect of her life, from her career to her relationships.

I first met Maria during a workshop I was conducting on self-worth and independence. Maria was a quiet participant, and her story unfolded as she shared her struggles with feeling inadequate despite her evident accomplishments.

It was clear that Maria's lack of confidence stemmed from her mother's overcompensating tendencies. Janet's well-meaning attempts to shield Maria from the world had inadvertently left her daughter feeling unprepared and insecure.

Through our sessions, we explored how Janet's own fears and anxieties had shaped Maria's self-perception. We worked on separating Maria's self-worth from her mother's influence.

Maria began to understand that her value wasn't dependent on her mother's approval or constant intervention. She started to take small steps toward independence, making decisions for herself and learning to embrace her own abilities without seeking validation from others.

Maria's solo trip to New York City was a turning point for her. Despite her usual anxiety about such ventures, she decided to go alone, which turned out to be both thrilling and challenging.

She tackled various tasks, from figuring out public transport to exploring new areas, all on her own. This trip made her realize that she could handle difficulties independently and that her worth wasn't dependent on her mother's constant presence.

This story highlights how a caregiver's attachment style can influence a child's self-worth. Janet's protective nature, although well-intentioned, had unintentionally hindered Maria's ability to develop independence.

By confronting these issues and discovering her own strengths, Maria was able to build a more confident and self-reliant sense of self.

EMBRACING YOUR STRENGTHS

You might think, "Strengths? Me? But I struggle with anxious attachment!" It's true that your attachment style affects how you feel, but it doesn't define who you are. Beneath the anxiety and fear, there are strengths like resilience, creativity, and compassion just waiting to be discovered.

Consider times when you've successfully handled challenges. Maybe you navigated a tough conversation gracefully, supported a friend with empathy, or pushed through a hard day with determination. These moments aren't just random; they show your strengths at work.

Perhaps you're great at solving problems, connecting with others, or being a reliable friend. These qualities are valuable and worth acknowledging. If identifying your strengths feels tough, that's okay. Years of focusing on insecurities can make it hard to see your own good traits.

Try reflecting on what brings you joy or tasks where you excel.

Asking trusted friends or family for their perspective can also help you see qualities you might have missed. Seeking support is a sign of strength, not weakness.

Once you identify your strengths, celebrate them. It might feel awkward at first, but it gets easier with practice. Start by acknowledging them to yourself, writing them down, or creating a "strength jar" where you keep notes about your positive traits. Share your strengths with others and appreciate your unique qualities, too.

As you get better at appreciating yourself, you'll notice a shift in your inner dialogue. The critical voice will quiet down, and you'll start to embrace yourself with kindness. Recognizing your worth means you won't need constant validation from others. You'll understand that you are enough, just as you are.

EXERCISE

Write a "Strengths Journal." Each day, list three strengths or positive qualities you possess. Reflect on how these strengths have helped you navigate life challenges and build resilience.

Find a Journal or Notebook:
- Choose a dedicated notebook, journal, or digital document where you will record your strengths daily.

Set Aside Time Each Day:
- Pick a specific time each day to write in your journal. It could be in the morning to start your day positively or in the evening to reflect on your day.

Write Today's Date:
- Start each entry with the date. This helps you track your progress over time.

List Three Strengths:

- Write down three positive qualities or strengths you possess. These could be traits like kindness, creativity, resilience, problem-solving skills, or empathy.
- Example:
    - Empathy
    - Creativity
    - Determination

Reflect on Each Strength:

- Next to each strength, write a brief note about how this quality has helped you in your life. Consider how it has supported you during challenging times or contributed to your personal growth.

Example:

- Empathy: "Empathy has allowed me to connect deeply with others and support friends during tough times."
- Creativity: "Creativity helped me find unique solutions to work problems and approach tasks with fresh perspectives."

Review and Appreciate:

- Take a moment to appreciate and acknowledge these strengths. Reflect on how recognizing them can boost your confidence and motivation.

Repeat Daily:

- Continue this exercise daily, adding new strengths or revisiting old ones. Over time, you'll build a comprehensive list of your positive qualities and see how they've contributed to your success and resilience.

Use the template below to help guide you to your strengths and qualities

Things I'm good at.....

What I like about my appearance....

I have helped others by........

What I value the most........

Compliments I have received

Challenges I have overcame...

Things that make me unique....

Times I made others happy.....

What strengths do I often overlook, and how can I recognize and celebrate them more?

____

____

____

____

How does embracing my strengths impact my self-worth and confidence?

____

____

____

____

Your task is not to seek for love, but merely to seek and find all the barriers within yourself that you have built against it.— Rumi

Chapter 6
THERAPEUTIC TOOLS
FOR HEALING

Nicole grew up in a small town near Lubbock, Texas, where the rhythms of rural life seemed calm, but her home life was anything but.

Her parents' affection was like a rollercoaster—sometimes warm and comforting, and other times cold and distant. Nicole's mother, Karen, was a dedicated and loving parent when her life was running smoothly.

She would spend hours helping Nicole with her schoolwork, attending her soccer games, and planning elaborate birthday parties.

But when Karen faced stress or personal difficulties, she would withdraw emotionally, leaving Nicole feeling abandoned and confused.

Nicole's father, Mark, was a different story. He was physically present but emotionally distant.

He worked long hours as a contractor, and when he was home, he was often preoccupied with work or his own personal interests.

Mark's interactions with Nicole were minimal, and his emotional availability was inconsistent. When he did engage with Nicole, it was often under the guise of being a stern authority figure rather than a nurturing parent.

As Nicole grew older, the mixed signals she received from her parents started to take a toll on her emotional well-being.

She excelled in school and was involved in several extracurricular activities, but she always felt an underlying sense of inadequacy. She would often seek validation from others, feeling that no matter how well she did, it was never quite enough.

I first met Nicole in my office after she had a series of relationship breakdowns. She described how she would sometimes push people away out of fear of being let down, and other times, she would cling to them desperately, fearing abandonment.

Her past was riddled with these conflicting emotions, stemming from her early experiences of inconsistent love and attention.

During our sessions, we went into Cognitive-Behavioral Therapy (CBT) to help Nicole challenge and reframe the negative beliefs she had formed about herself.

We worked on identifying and changing the automatic thoughts that led her to seek constant approval and validation from others. This process helped Nicole start to see her worth independently of her parents' fluctuating affections.

We also explored Attachment-Focused Therapy, where Nicole learned to understand and address the impact of her parents' inconsistent parenting on her adult relationships.

Through this therapy, she was able to confront and process her feelings of abandonment and develop healthier ways to form and maintain secure connections.

CHANGING THOUGHTS
AND BEHAVIORS

So, how does Cognitive Behavioral Therapy (CBT) work? At its core, CBT is about understanding how our thoughts, feelings, and behaviors are all connected.

When you're dealing with anxious attachment, your thoughts can be very negative and catastrophic, like "They don't love me anymore" or "I'm going to be alone forever."

These thoughts then lead to strong emotions such as anxiety and fear, which drive behaviors like clinging or withdrawing. It creates a cycle that CBT aims to break.

CBT helps by teaching you to spot and challenge these distorted thoughts. Think of it like those carnival funhouse mirrors that twist your reflection; anxious attachment can warp your view of reality, making you focus on your flaws and fears rather than your strengths and worth.

CBT helps you become a detective of your own thoughts.

You learn to identify patterns like "all-or-nothing thinking" (seeing things as either perfect or terrible) or "mind reading" (assuming you know what others are thinking without proof). By spotting these distortions, you can question them with evidence and logic, which helps you see yourself and your relationships more clearly.

But CBT goes beyond just changing your thoughts. It also helps you adjust behaviors that keep you stuck in this anxious cycle. For instance, if you frequently text your partner for reassurance, CBT guides you to recognize these behaviors and find healthier ways to cope, such as setting boundaries, practicing self-soothing techniques, or doing things that build your self-esteem.

It's like learning a new dance. At first, it may feel awkward and challenging, but with practice and support from a therapist, you'll gradually become more comfortable and confident in navigating your relationships and emotions. CBT isn't a quick fix—it requires time, effort, and dedication to change deeply rooted patterns of thinking and behavior.

ATTACHMENT-FOCUSED THERAPY

Attachment-Focused Therapy (AFT) isn't about placing blame or dwelling on the past. Instead, it's a journey of self-discovery and healing.

You'll look at how your early experiences have shaped your beliefs about yourself and others. With a skilled therapist's guidance, you'll learn to challenge these beliefs and replace them with healthier, more empowering ones.

A common misconception is that therapy is solely about revisiting painful memories. While exploring your past is part of it, AFT focuses on creating new experiences that build secure attachments. Think of it as learning the new "language" of healthy relationships.

Your therapist acts as a secure base, offering a safe space for you to express your emotions and explore vulnerabilities. This therapeutic relationship helps you develop a more positive sense of self and a greater capacity for trust, like having a personal trainer for your emotional well-being.

AFT also emphasizes emotional regulation. If you're often overwhelmed by anxiety or fear in your relationships, your therapist will teach you techniques to manage these emotions more effectively. Imagine it as installing a dimmer switch for your feelings, so you can adjust their intensity as needed.

As you progress, you'll notice changes in your relationship patterns. You might communicate more openly, set boundaries with greater confidence, and understand your partner's needs better. This newfound awareness will help you approach your relationships with greater empathy and compassion.

EXERCISE

Use CBT to challenge anxious thoughts. Identify a specific thought pattern related to anxious attachment (e.g., "I'm unlovable"), and work through a cognitive restructuring exercise to replace it with a healthier, more balanced thought.

Steps:

Identify a Negative Thought:

- Choose a specific thought related to your anxious attachment. For example, "I'm unlovable" or "No one will ever want me."

Write Down the Thought:

- On a piece of paper or in a journal, write down the negative thought exactly as you think it.

Examine the Evidence:

- Ask yourself: What evidence supports this thought? What evidence contradicts it? For example, if your thought is "I'm unlovable," list any positive experiences or relationships that show you are indeed lovable.

Challenge the Thought:

- Consider if there are any cognitive distortions (e.g., all-or-nothing thinking, overgeneralization) present in this thought. Challenge these distortions by finding a more balanced perspective.

Create a Balanced Thought:

- Based on the evidence and challenges, create a more balanced, positive thought. For example, replace "I'm unlovable" with "I have qualities that people appreciate, and I am capable of forming meaningful relationships."

Test the New Thought:

- Reflect on how the new balanced thought makes you feel compared to the original negative thought. Does it make you feel more positive or hopeful?

Reinforce the New Thought:

- Repeat the balanced thought to yourself regularly, especially when you notice the old negative thought creeping in. Practice it until it starts to feel more natural.

Reflect on Your Progress:

- Take a moment to reflect on any changes in your feelings or behaviors since using this new thought. Note any improvements in your emotional well-being or relationships.

Use the template below as a guide.

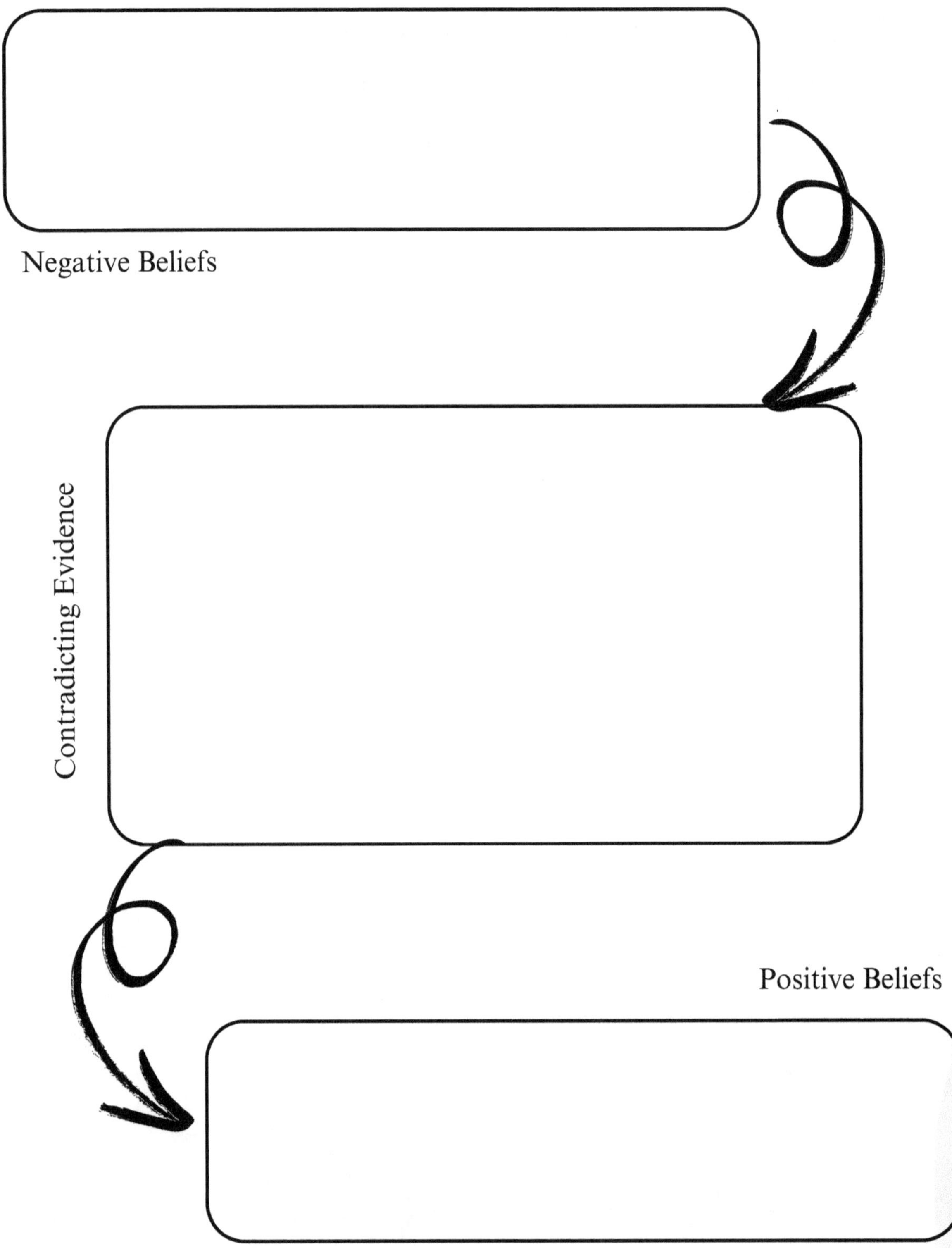

Negative Beliefs
Contradicting Evidence
Positive Beliefs

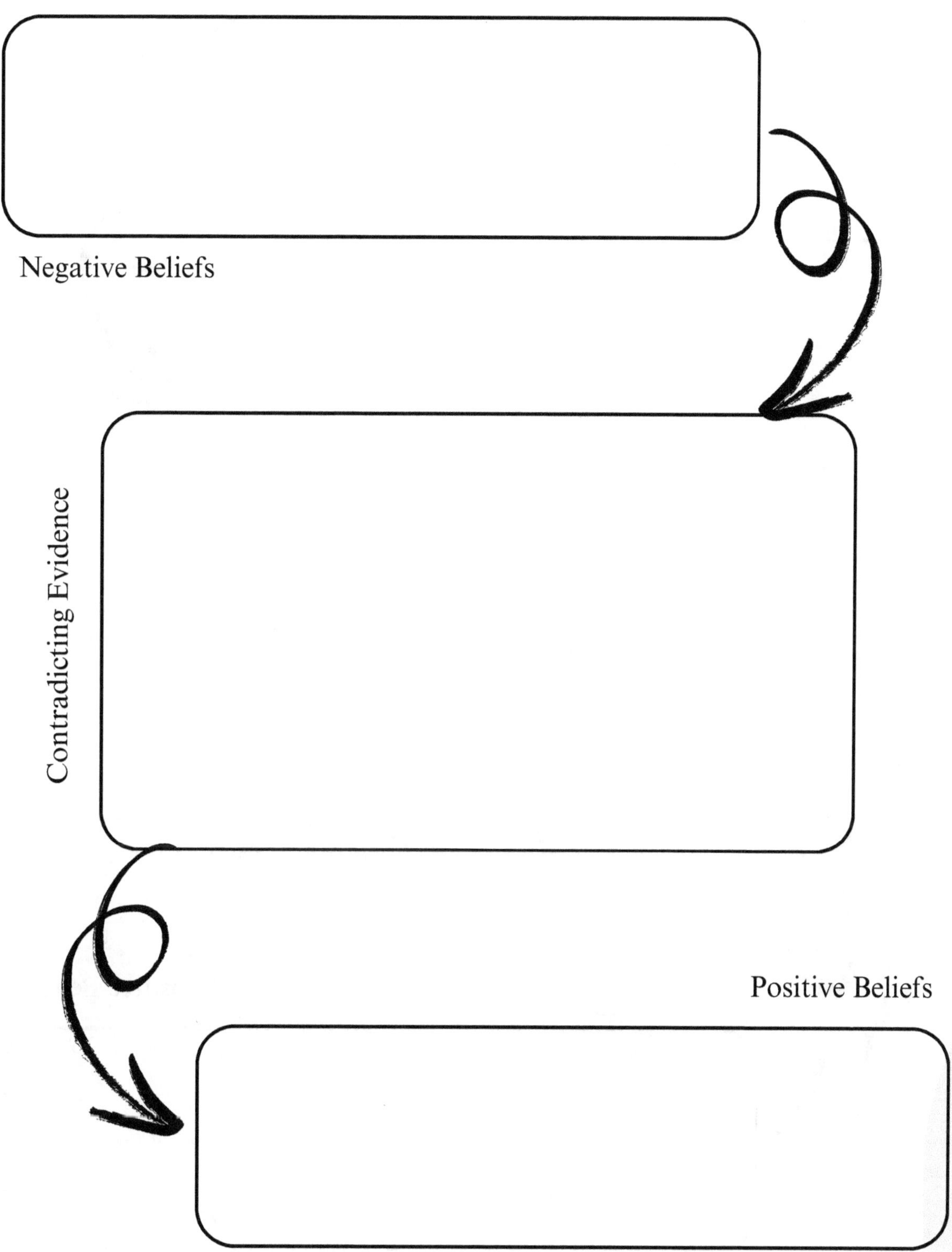

Negative Beliefs
Contradicting Evidence
Positive Beliefs

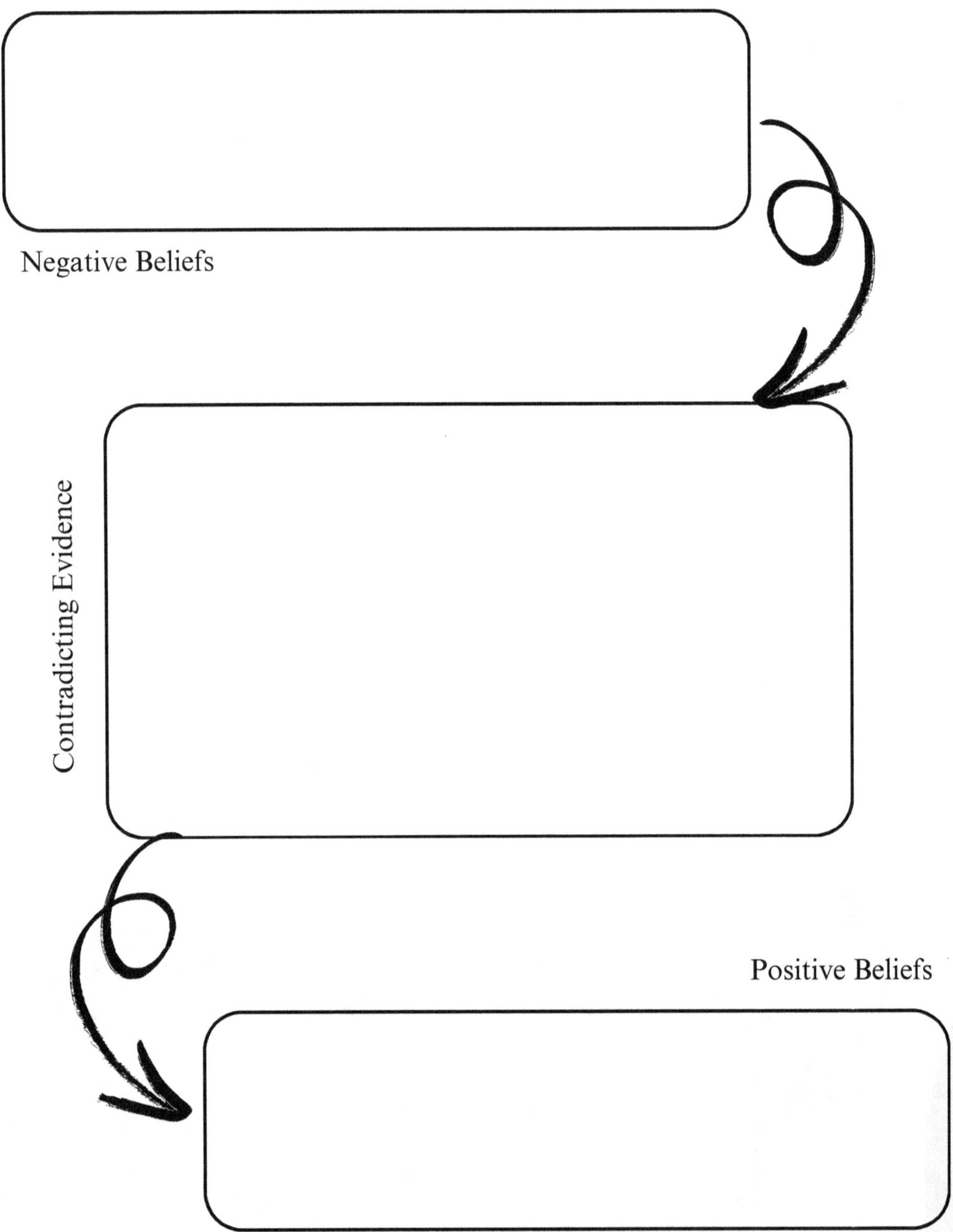
Negative Beliefs
Contradicting Evidence
Positive Beliefs

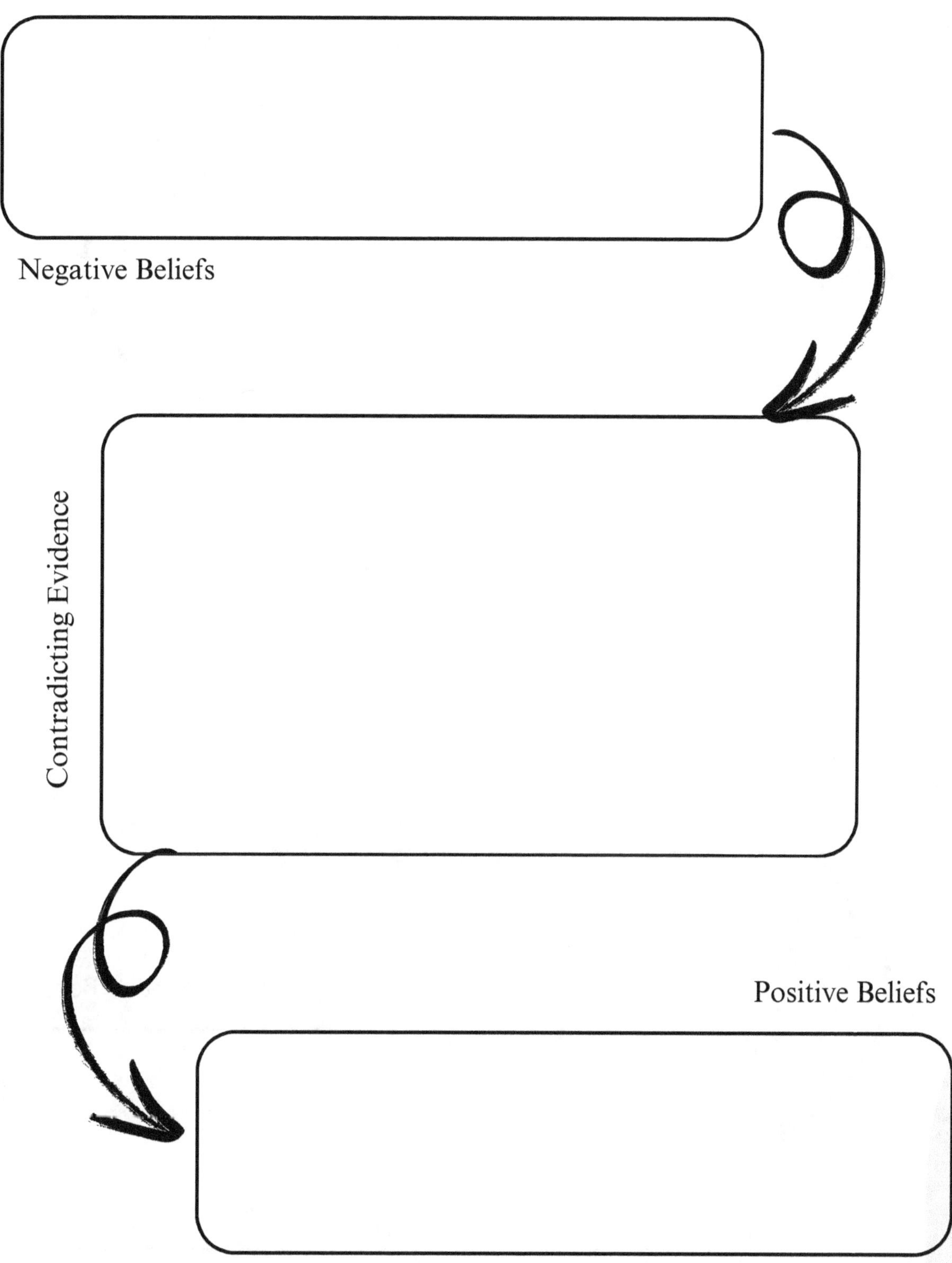

Negative Beliefs
Contradicting Evidence
Positive Beliefs

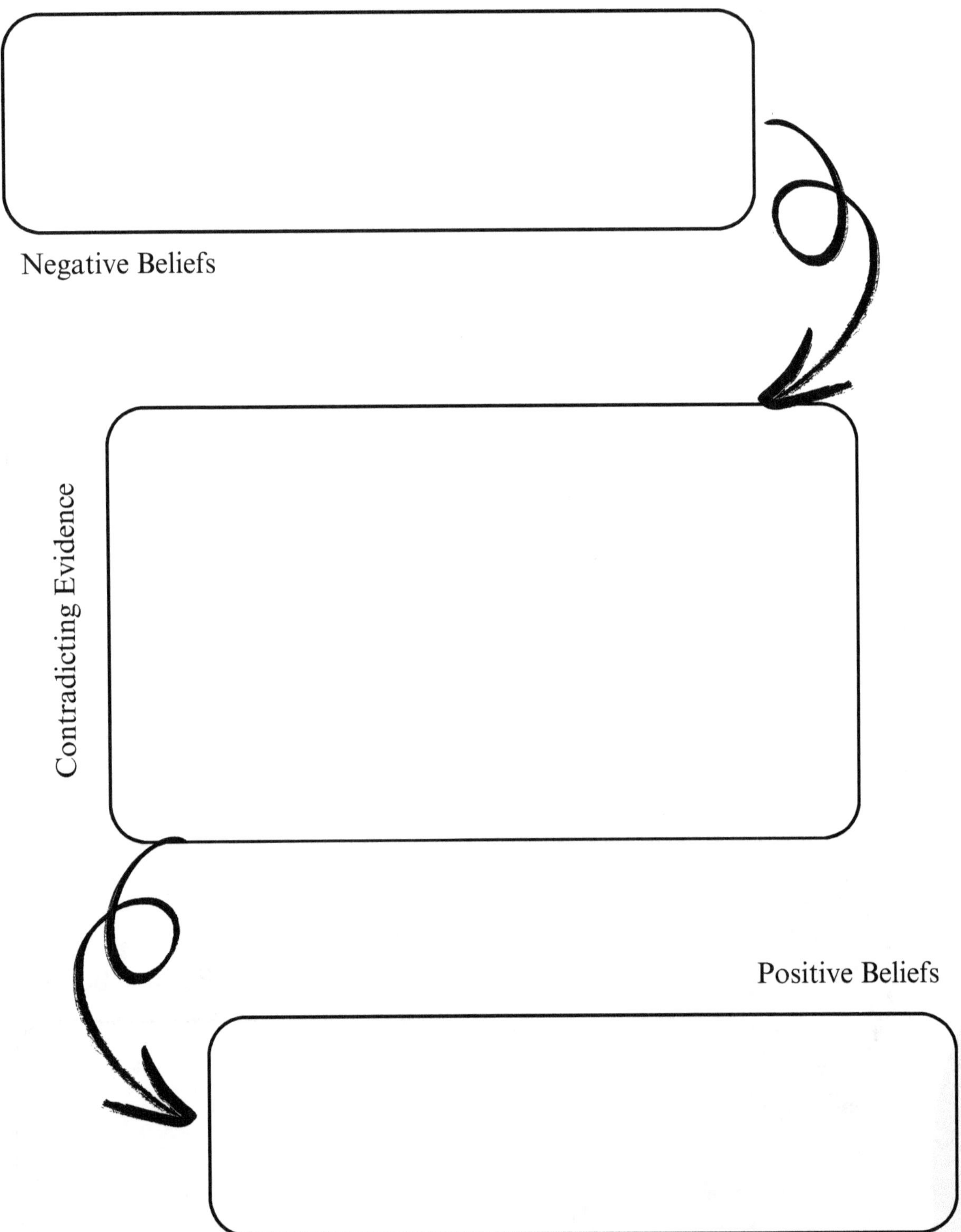

Negative Beliefs
Contradicting Evidence
Positive Beliefs

What automatic thoughts arise when I feel insecure or anxious in relationships?

____

____

____

____

____

How can I challenge these thoughts using CBT techniques?

____

____

____

____

Our greatest attachment is to the beliefs we have about love.— Marianne Williamson

Chapter 7

EMBRACING A SECURE FUTURE

After confronting your past and embracing the wounds of your inner child, you're now ready to step into a future that's built on security and fulfillment.

This isn't about erasing your history; those experiences have made you the strong person you are today. Instead, it's about rewriting the story—creating a future where your past no longer controls your present or what lies ahead.

This chapter doesn't provide strict steps to follow. Rather, it invites you to explore what's possible when you let go of fear and insecurity.

It encourages you to trust in your inner strength and resilience, which have grown throughout your healing journey.

One of the biggest shifts you'll notice is a stronger sense of self-trust. As you've learned to care for your inner child and manage your emotions, you've developed a deep well of inner strength. This self-trust will guide you toward choices that reflect your needs and values, without the constant need for outside validation to feel worthy or loved.

As your self-trust grows, so will the quality of your relationships. The desperate need for reassurance that once fueled your interactions will lessen. You'll be drawn to people who value and respect you for who you are, not as a reflection of their own insecurities. These deeper connections will be built on mutual trust, open communication, and shared values.

The journey to a secure future won't always be smooth. There will be setbacks, moments of doubt, and times when old fears resurface. But remember, you are not defined by your past. You are constantly evolving and learning. Every setback is a chance to grow stronger and reinforce the resilience you've built.

LETTING GO
OF FEAR

You may find yourself struggling with jealousy, overanalyzing every word and action, or engaging in people-pleasing behaviors to avoid conflict.

These responses, while completely understandable, come from a place of fear. And that fear, unfortunately, can sabotage the very thing you want most—building healthy, fulfilling relationships.

Letting go of fear doesn't mean pretending it doesn't exist. It means acknowledging its presence, understanding where it comes from, and deciding that it won't dictate your actions.

Your fears, though real, might not accurately reflect reality. It's about daring to believe you are worthy of love and that your relationships can be sources of joy and security—not just anxiety and heartache.

One of the most transformative ways to release fear is to embrace vulnerability. This means showing up authentically in your relationships, even when it feels uncomfortable or risky. It means expressing your needs honestly, sharing your insecurities openly, and allowing yourself to be truly seen.

Vulnerability can feel especially daunting for someone with anxious attachment. It exposes you to potential rejection or hurt. But at the same time, it opens the door to real connection, intimacy, and love.

When you allow yourself to be vulnerable, you give others the permission to do the same, fostering an environment of genuine understanding and mutual support.

Think of it this way: Imagine holding a ball of tightly wound yarn. That ball represents your heart, wrapped up and shielded by layers of fear. As you slowly start to unravel it, you begin to reveal more of yourself. It might feel awkward or uncomfortable at first, but as you continue, that yarn becomes a long thread, capable of reaching out and creating connections with others.

Unraveling fear isn't always easy. There will be times when you're tempted to retreat and wind that yarn back up. But if you persist and keep choosing vulnerability over fear, you'll find the reward—deeper, more meaningful connections—is worth it.

Letting go of fear and embracing vulnerability allows you to break free from the limitations of anxious attachment. You stop trying to control your relationships and instead let them develop naturally. You learn to trust yourself, your partner, and the process of love itself.

This doesn't mean you'll never feel anxious or insecure again—those feelings are part of the human experience. But as you strengthen your sense of self-worth and learn to trust the strength of your connections, these feelings will no longer control you. You'll face them with courage, knowing that they don't define you or your relationships.

CREATING HEALTHY RELATIONSHIPS

For those of us with anxious attachment, reaching out for support can feel as inviting as a root canal.

The fear of rejection, the vulnerability hangover, and that nagging voice telling us we're "too much" can easily send us running back to the safety of our comfort zones. Curling up and binge-watching our favorite shows seems like the better option, right?

But here's the truth: isolating ourselves only feeds the anxious attachment monster.

It reinforces those deeply ingrained beliefs that we're not worthy of love and that we're better off alone. It's like trying to put out a fire by pouring gasoline on it.

So how do we escape this cycle of self-imposed isolation and create a supportive network that actually supports us? Let's break it down into actionable steps:

Redefine "Supportive Network"

Forget the picture-perfect social media ideal of a large group of friends always available for brunch. A supportive network doesn't have to be big or perfectly curated.

It could be just a few close friends, a therapist, a family member, or even an online community that gets what you're going through. Remember, it's about quality over quantity.

Start Small

If the idea of pouring your heart out makes you want to hide under a blanket, start small. Reach out to one person you trust—a friend who's a good listener, a family member who's been there for you, or a therapist who specializes in attachment issues.

Open up about your struggles and see how they respond. If they offer genuine empathy and support, that's a great sign you've found someone worth keeping close.

Be Clear About Your Needs

Anxious folks often wish others could read their minds, but unfortunately, that's not how it works. Instead of hoping people will automatically know what you need, be clear and specific.

Whether you need someone to simply listen, offer advice, or just send a funny meme to cheer you up, let them know. And don't be afraid to ask for exactly what you need.

Embrace Vulnerability

Yes, I know—this one's a tough pill to swallow. But vulnerability is the gateway to real connection. Sharing your fears, insecurities, and struggles with the right people creates authentic relationships.

It might be terrifying at first, but the relief that comes from not having to hide is worth it. And you might be surprised how much others relate to your experiences.

Reciprocate Support

Relationships are a two-way street. Offer support in return—whether it's a listening ear, a word of encouragement, or just being present.

Not only does this strengthen your relationships, but it also reminds you that you have value to offer others, too.

Don't Be Afraid to Cut Ties

Not everyone deserves a spot in your support network. If someone consistently invalidates your feelings, gives you unsolicited advice, or makes you feel worse, it's okay to distance yourself.

You have the right to curate your support system to include people who uplift and support you, rather than dragging you down.

E
X
E
R
C
I
S
E

Write a "Manifesto for a Secure Future." Outline the type of relationships you want to cultivate, the person you want to become, and how you will continue to let go of fear and embrace trust in yourself and others.

Step 1: Set the Scene

Find a quiet and comfortable place where you won't be interrupted. Take a few deep breaths to center yourself, and imagine you're about to write a declaration for your future. This is your personal manifesto—a guiding statement for the life you want to create.

Step 2: Reflect on Your Ideal Relationships

Start by thinking about the kind of relationships you want in your life (romantic, friendships, family, etc.). Ask yourself:

- What qualities do I want these relationships to have (e.g., trust, support, mutual respect)?
- How do I want to feel in these relationships (e.g., secure, valued, loved)?
- What boundaries will I need to set to maintain healthy relationships?

Step 3: Envision Your Future Self

Now, reflect on the person you want to become. Ask yourself:

- What personal traits do I want to cultivate (e.g., confidence, compassion, resilience)?
- How will I show up for myself and others?
- What will my life look like when I am living in alignment with my values?

Step 4: Let Go of Fear and Embrace Trust

Consider how you will release fear and build trust. Ask yourself:

- What fears do I need to let go of (e.g., fear of abandonment, rejection)?
- How will I begin to trust myself and others more?
- What practices will I adopt to reinforce this trust (e.g., self-care, mindfulness, open communication)?

Step 5: Write Your Manifesto

Put it all together. Write a clear and positive statement that captures your vision for your relationships and future self. Your manifesto might include affirmations, intentions, or promises to yourself.

Example:

"I am cultivating relationships built on trust, love, and mutual respect. I am becoming a person who is confident, compassionate, and secure in my worth. I release fear and embrace trust in myself and those around me. I am committed to living a life aligned with my values, filled with joy, peace, and meaningful connections."

Step 6: Review and Revisit

After writing your manifesto, read it aloud to yourself. Notice how it makes you feel. Keep this document somewhere accessible, and revisit it whenever you need a reminder of the future you are working towards.

What fears am I still holding onto, and how are they preventing me from building secure relationships?

____

____

____

____

How can I begin to trust myself more in navigating relationships and life decisions?

____

____

____

____

Thank You!

Thank you so much for purchasing and reading *Anxious Attachment Workbook for Women*. Your time and trust in this journey mean the world to me. I hope this book has brought you closer to healing and growth.

If you found it helpful, I would truly appreciate it if you could leave a review on Amazon—your feedback helps others discover this resource.

As a special thank you, please scan the QR code for a bonus gift!

With gratitude,

Isabella Cruz

All of our attachments carry with them the potential for pain, because life is unpredictable.— Thich Nhat Hanh